THE POST-WAR REVIVAL OF AMATEUR BUILT AIRCRAFT BEING THE STORY OF THE LUTON MINOR

Arthur W. J. G. Ord-Hume

Don Ellis, husband of Sandown airfield-owner ex-ATA Mary Wilkins, flies close in G-AFGE, his BAC Swallow to capture an air-to-air snapshot of Luton Minor G-ASAA. Don and I used to do some pretty close-up formation flights at times, flying to nearby air-shows and holding station during some series of admittedly gentle turns and changes of direction. It was all great fun.

Stenlake Publishing Ltd

© 2024 Arthur W. J. G. Ord-Hume
First Published in the United Kingdom, 2024
Stenlake Publishing Limited
54-58 Mill Square, Catrine, KA5 6RD
www.stenlake.co.uk

ISBN 978-1-84033-972-7

Printed by
P2D Books, 1 Newlands Rd,
Westoning, Bedford, MK45 5LD

An example of what can be achieved when you try hard enough! This fine example of the LA.4a was built by D J Gaskin in Bexley, Kent, with an Ardem converted VW engine. The colour scheme is white and red.

Introduction

A visit to the annual fly-in of the Light Aircraft Association is a true eye-opener when one sees so many home-made aircraft together on the grass. Such a variety of types, styles, colours… Line after line of amateur-built aircraft park in serried rows up to a thousand and more in total, each the creation of an enthusiast with a passion for building and flying their own aircraft. Can there be that number – *really*?

These fine aircraft, all turned out in spotless order, point out clearly the difference between the two similar words in the English language – amateur (as in amateur-made) and amateurish (as is amateur-looking). Where the latter is a derogatory term for something slipshod and looking as if made without skill, the amateur-made aircraft often demonstrates a quality of finish that would shame many a factory-produced aeroplane. The amateur, who, by definition, does not get paid for his work, therefore can spend as long as he wants on getting it absolutely right as distinct from 'just right'. The amateur seeks his reward in satisfaction, not an hourly-rate pay-packet.

The home-built aeroplane is, consequently, pretty high up in the hierarchy of quality of build, finish and presentation.

Home-builts are not just flivvers for local flights; single-seaters for a bit of air experience. Today's home-made aeroplane can be a two-seater or even what the Americans call a four-place – a cabin with seats for four people. And the materials of construction have moved on from wood and fabric to plastics and metal, composites and other high-grade materials once considered out of the reach of the garden-shed dabbler.

As for journeys undertaken, Frenchman Henri Mignet managed to fly his home-made *Pou-du-Ciel* over the Alps in the mid-1930s. In more recent times, we have seen home-builts fly the Atlantic and even circumnavigate the globe. Many of the amateur aircraft of today can happily rival production types when it comes to achievements in distance and altitude.

But it wasn't always like that. In fact, probably through an oversight in legislation, by the outbreak of the 1939-45 war, home-made aircraft were virtually illegal. There was no way that a home-built aircraft could qualify for a regular Certificate of Airworthiness – the ubiquitous C of A – and the Permit to Fly system was restricted to special designated flight by normally-certified aircraft, usually for one flight to a maintenance base where a C of A overhaul could be carried out for renewal.

The few remaining owners of pre-war aircraft that once operated happily on a Permit to Fly found themselves grounded after the war was over. The aviation magazines of the time were full of letters from frustrated owners of pre-war small aeroplanes that had once operated on the Permit system and were now grounded by officialdom. Put simply, there was no legislation to cover these aircraft. They had metaphorically fallen through a gap in the folds of aviation's rulebook.

So what is this book about? I have myself struggled to define what the real subject is, let alone what title it should masquerade under. It's about several things and I hope I have been successful in rolling them all into one. It is first and foremost the story of the fight to re-establish the British home-built aircraft movement after the 1939-45 war. It also relates the story of the Luton Minor light aircraft and, in so doing, additionally records the history of Luton Aircraft Ltd and the post-war Phoenix Aircraft Ltd. The little wooden aeroplane in this story was to play a now-forgotten part in developing the Popular Flying Association, now the Light Aircraft Association.

While America did not have the same restrictions as we did, it founded its equivalent of our PFA (which can trace its origins back to 1946) in 1953. Openly based on our PFA's aims and objectives, this was called the Experimental Aircraft Association. The publication of a regular series of articles on aircraft woodwork in the EAA magazine, initially called *The Experimenter* but, later, *Sport Aviation*, boosted the amateur aviation goal and encouraged many Americans to build and fly their own aircraft.

All this was under the leadership of EAA founder Paul Poberezny (1922-2013). Paul was a great leader and supercharged a small but established American home-building movement. For my part in this, I received an EAA Trophy in 1961 and numerous 'individual achievement award' certificates. The loss of Paul was enormous but the great enterprise he started survives and is still expanding.

Setting the Scene

Let's not duck the issue here! Throughout the history of flight there have always been home-made aeroplanes. The pioneers were all essentially home-builders. Since the beginning of aviation, amateur aircraft constructors have lurked somewhere in the background, usually without causing a ripple in history or much more than a brief reference in the history books.

By the first quarter of the 20th century, however, aviation was, to a great extent, a leap of faith beyond the average UK mortal. This reticence to take a step into the technology of flight was maybe no more than a British thing because Americans, for example, had been dabbling in aviation at all levels all through history, mainly without too much in the way of success and without excessive interference from authority.

The average UK enthusiast, however, tended to stop short of actually trying to make an aeroplane.

All this changed in 1935 with the arrival of Frenchman Henri Mignet on the scene. Heralded by the perhaps unfortunate assertion that 'anyone who can knock together a packing case can build a plane', Mignet's *Pou-du-Ciel* became the inspiration for the rapid onset of what became known in Britain as the *Flying Flea* craze.

Thanks to the enthusiastic encouragement of the daily press which viewed such events with a 1930s newspaper-man's newsworthy eye, people all over the country eagerly took to Mignet and his design with an almost religious fervour. Backed by a

Things were different in Britain. The immediate post-war years were not conducive to the amateur builder here. What with continued rationing of food and other essential domestic commodities not to mention increasing austerity that seemed at variance with winning the war, any activity outside that necessary for survival was seen as a luxury.

This slim book relates how it all changed and how one pre-war aircraft design was revived to become the first UK post-war design for amateur construction. It was a long and curious struggle and to tell it properly one has to go back to 1935, a time when we were only just recovering economically from the infamous Wall Street Crash of October 1929 that heralded the Depression that was to last virtually up to the start of the Second World War.

Today it's hard to believe but the Luton Minor played a vital part in the development of the post-war amateur aircraft construction movement here in Britain. Without the Luton Minor's part in the history of the second half of the 20th century, things would have been a lot different – or should I say worse!

This, then, is the story of a one shoestring pre-war design that found itself in the curious position of bridging the 1939-45 war through the good fortune of happening to possess the right paperwork in an age when paperwork was king, and the efforts of a handful of enthusiasts who took on the mighty ones in Whitehall who tried to stop them from flying.

The post-war Luton LA.4a Minor was a neat, robust looking aircraft. This one was fitted with a converted VW flat-four engine.

newly-formed organisation given a grand name – The Air League of the British Empire – supported by an English translation of the Frenchman's 'how to do it' book sponsored by the Air League, British-made Flying Fleas were soon being built all over the country.

The monthly magazine *Practical Mechanics* eagerly commissioned a series of articles describing construction in detail. This form of design endorsement unleashed a torrent of enthusiasm in otherwise normal men as, up and down the land, a hitherto dormant urge to make an aeroplane saw fulfilment. People started building Fleas. Some were individual projects, others 'club' efforts where a number of people got together and each contributed to completing the whole.

But there was a problem. All aircraft operate in what is termed a 'flight envelope' which, very briefly, means that they have a wide margin of flight safety and ability represented by a smooth curve like the profile of a wave. If the top is the peak of performance, there is still a degree of flying safety and ability either side near the top of that wave profile, albeit with gradually diminishing performance.

Mignet, on the other hand, produced a design that did not have so much as a performance curve as a sharp performance *peak*. He was just extremely lucky to have hit the very top of that profile with his prototype. A small deviation either side, however, spelled potential disaster.

Mignet, hailed as a genius, was a real amateur and not an aerodynamicist. Initially he didn't appreciate this basic fact which is why the story of the Flying Flea ended up as controversial. In short, the Flying Flea had a basic and serious aerodynamic flaw. To adjust the position of the Centre of Gravity (CG), one was encouraged to move the front of its two wings forwards or backwards.

Now the Flying Flea was best described as a super-staggered tailless biplane. If the front wing, which was pivoted so that its angle of incidence could be controlled by the pilot's control column, overlapped the rear wing, pulling the stick back to climb effectively made the front wing act as an aerodynamic slot for the rear wing. This actually increased the lift of the rear wing, pushing the nose downwards.

The result, for the pilot, was the exact opposite of what he expected. It usually ended in an inverted landing, sometimes with fatal results

This peculiarity of control and its true cause was only really isolated when a full-sized aircraft was placed in the wind-tunnel at the National Physical Laboratory and calibrated under the strict research centre conditions. After that, the Air Ministry, licensing authority for all things that flew, refused to issue any more flying permits for Flying Fleas. Not exactly banned, but ostensibly grounded for good. Significantly, several aerodynamically re-engineered Fleas were allowed to fly after this edict.

Nobody knows for sure how many Flying Fleas were built across the country. At least 108 were registered but a large number were built and some actually flown without any markings. It is thought that at least 250 were built or under construction across the country. The news of the cancellation of any authority to fly them was thus a huge blow to the fledgling amateur aircraft construction market.

This came as a shock to the many hundreds of people across the country who were building Fleas or who were actually attempting to fly them. Tempted by the new concept of the common man's aeroplane, there existed a number of people nationwide who wanted to take advantage of this new opportunity of building their own real aeroplane. It was an open invitation for some aircraft design entrepreneur to capitalise on the situation…

The demise of the Flying Flea left doors wide open for a safe successor to the nascent build-it-yourself market. Several contenders came forward offering conventional designs such as the Perman Parasol, Broughton-Blaney Broughton and Dart Kitten. These were also products of extremely small companies that would best be termed one-man bands. Dart Aircraft was the brainchild of glider-designer A R Weyl while Perman had previously produced Fleas and kits of parts for the Flea.

It fell to a young glider designer named Latimer-Needham to initiate what would be a sea-change in the history of the home-made aeroplane.

Enter a British designer

Cecil Hugh Latimer-Needham (1900-1975) was born in London's Walthamstow and educated at Berkhamsted School and University College London. He joined the Royal Flying Corps in France during 1918, served with the Army of Occupation and, in 1919, transferred to the Royal Air Force, becoming Educational Officer based at RAF Halton until 1935. During the 1920s he was involved in the design of the Halton Mayfly biplane for the Halton Aero Club, a group which he had been responsible for forming in 1925. This was followed by the Halton Minus monoplane and the unfinished Halton Meteor twin-engined tailless aircraft.

An interest in gliding led to his being an early pioneer of the sport in Britain designing the first all-British glider called the Albatross, built for him by R F Dagnall & Company in Guildford in 1930. He went on to found the Dunstable Sailplane Company. Appointed the first Chairman of the Technical Committee of the British Gliding Association he advised on the design of both powered and non-powered flight.

He left the RAF in 1935 to form his own company, Luton Aircraft, at Barton-in-the-Clay, a village in Bedfordshire, bordering Hertfordshire. A shoestring outfit with limited resources, he designed a powered sailplane called the Buzzard and then, recognising the limitations of the Flying Flea, attempted to make a safer version with an elongated fuselage, two wings arranged like those of the Flea in tandem, but with a conventional tail unit and control system. He called this the Luton LA.2 Minor.

With a 32 hp inverted Vee Anzani engine on the front, this did not fly well and following several high-speed hops, the designer concluded that the rear wing was redundant since it created more drag than lift.

The company did not remain at Barton-in-the-Clay for long and in 1936 shifted to Gerrards Cross where, at the tiny village of Tatling End on what was then called the Oxford Road, it had set up a workshop behind a motoring garage owned and operated by Latimer-Needham's brother. At the nearby Denham Aerodrome newly created by surgeon John Myles Bickerton (1894-1977) the prototype Luton Minor, now registered G-AEPD, made its first flight. By this time the aircraft had shed its rear wing and reverted to a more conventional lightplane layout.

Publicity in the aeronautical press inspired a letter from fellow aerodynamicist, Henry Braid Irving (1889-1961) who had just published a paper on the claimed aerodynamic advantages of converging tapered wings in biplane form. In a letter to Luton Aircraft Ltd dated December 13th, 1936, Irving proposed trying his novel biplane wings on the LA.2 to evaluate what he believed to be the advantageous slow-flying characteristics of his wing format.

Unfortunately for Irving, the tiny Luton company was not sufficiently well-breeched to undertake any such experimental work and so the Irving overlapping, tapered wings went untried. Meanwhile the aeroplane, now known as the LA.3 Minor, continued to undergo trials.

The prototype Luton LA.2 Minor was a super-staggered biplane with a normal tailplane with elevator and rudder as seen here in this hangar shot taken at Barton-in-the-Clay. The aircraft is resting on trestles to keep it in a level flight position with the wheels just off the ground. While the aft part of the Warren-girder braced fuselage was fabric covered, the forward part was plywood skinned. The later machine, as published in the magazine *Practical Mechanics*, had a fuselage that was fully skinned in plywood.

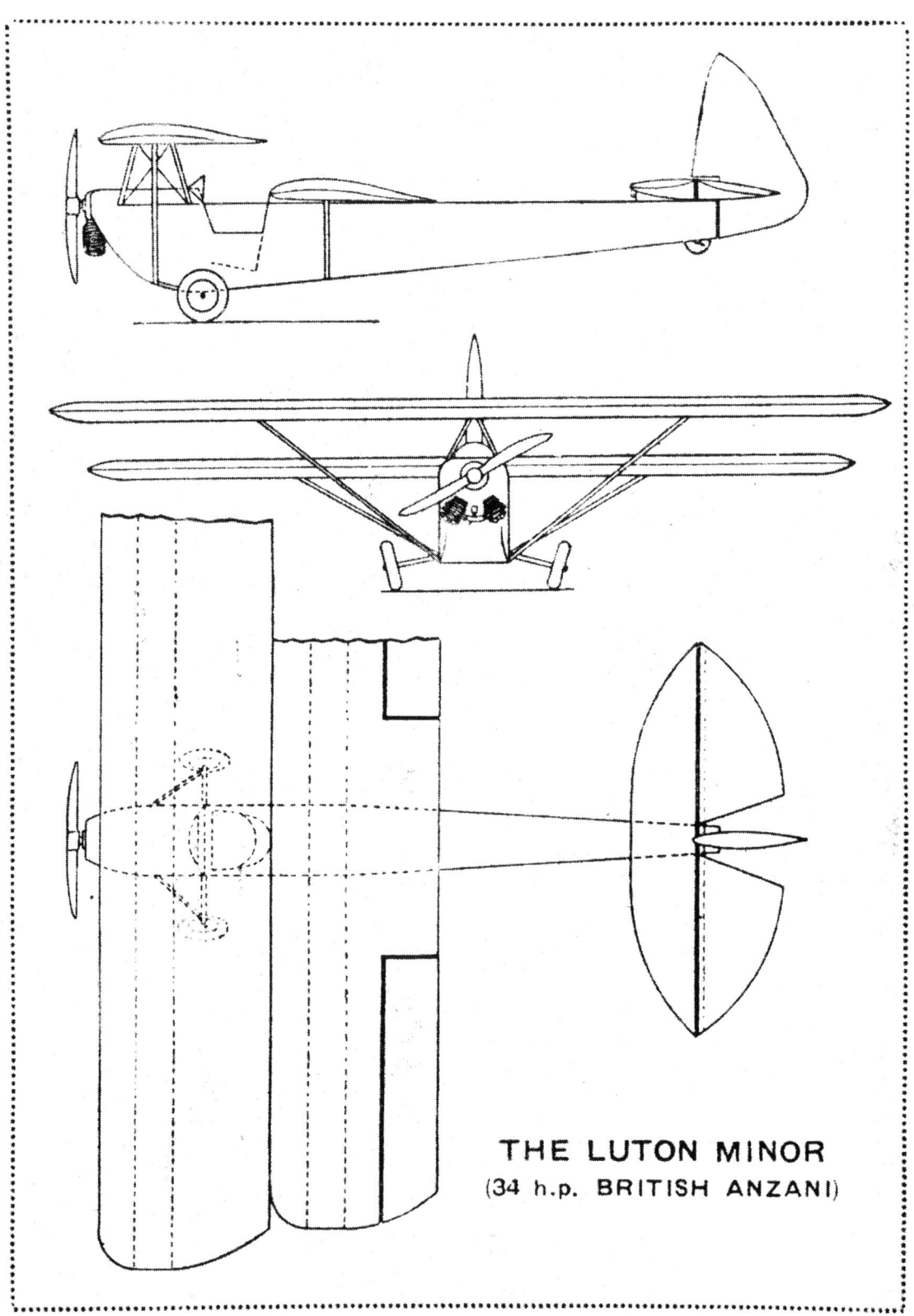

The first news of the Luton Minor came just after the firm moved from Barton-in-the-Clay to Gerrards Cross. Under the headline 'Recruits for the Light Brigade, New Approaches to the "Ultra-light" Problem', *Flight* of December 10th, 1936, published this three-view drawing with an article that opened with the observation: 'Produced, according to Luton Aircraft, Ltd., of Gerrards Cross, Bucks, to provide an essentially safe aeroplane which may take the place of the *Pou-du-Ciel*, the Luton Minor will eventually be available for amateur construction. Safety in flight has been the primary consideration in the design, but cheapness and simplicity have been kept very close in view. The makers claim that the Minor is capable of cross-country flights, as opposed, presumably, to leisurely circuits of the aerodrome on a quiet summer day'.

The next development was styled the Luton LA.3 Minor. Perhaps to prove that this one really was going to fly, it was registered G-AEPD. Here the prototype prepares for take-off. Gone is the rear wing and it looks a little more like an aeroplane. Note the fuselage form, the Vee-shaped lift struts and the Flying Flea-type undercarriage. The engine is the Luton Anzani inverted Vee twin.

Here is a snapshot of the first really flyable Luton Minor in the skies for the first time.

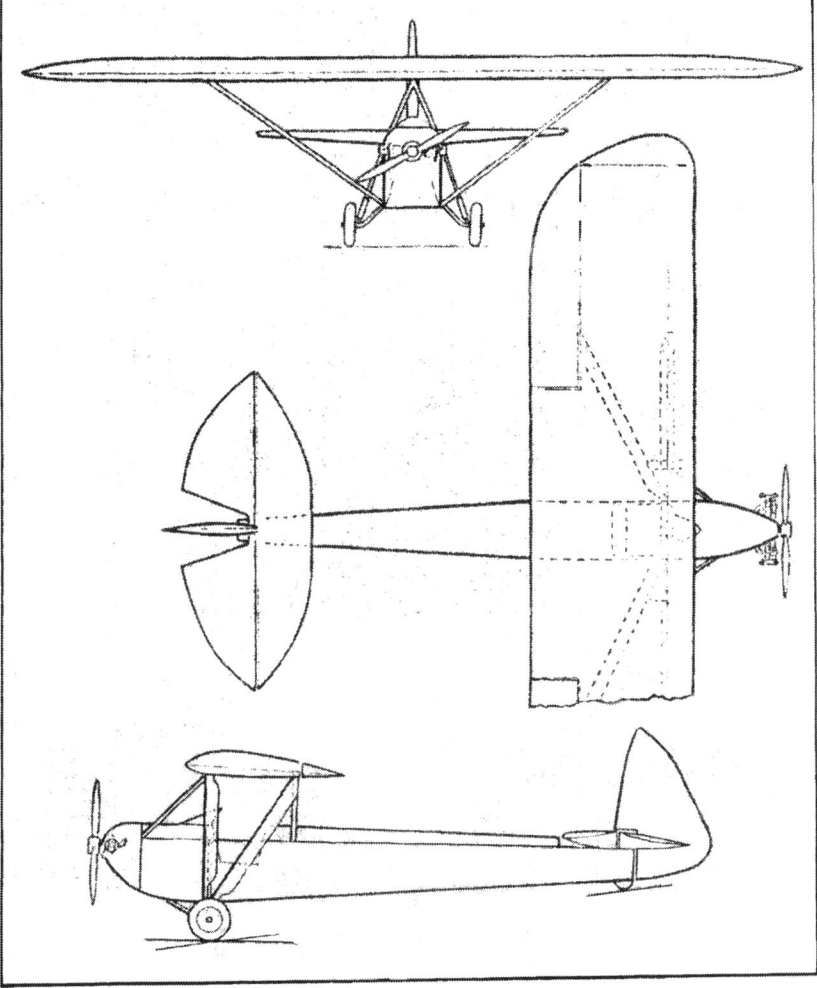

In the issue of *Flight* for March 11th, 1937, under the heading 'Lively Lightweight', was printed an article on the Luton Minor 'in its latest form' illustrated with a picture of the V-strutted parasol G-AEPD and a close-up of Latimer-Needham leaning into the cockpit with the Anzani engine running. The three-view drawing is accompanied by the comment that 'In production a [Douglas] Sprite flat twin will be fitted, but any engine of about 30 hp is an alternative'. In fact, there is no record of the Sprite being fitted to a Minor: it would have been a little on the weak side. Observe the shape of the tailplane.

Prototype Luton LA.3 Minor reveals some Flying Flea derivatives, namely the big rudder and the through-axle undercarriage. Powered by the Luton-Anzani engine of about 35 hp, the V-strutted G-AEPD was not a particularly good flyer but demonstrated enough promise to encourage the development of the more familiar LA.4 Minor, G-AFBP, that followed.

The project received a boost when the magazine *Practical Mechanics*, edited by F J Camm, pressed Latimer-Needham for a series of articles on how to build the Luton Minor.

Frederick James Camm (1895–1959) was an interesting man. The brother of the Hawker Hurricane designer Sydney Camm, he was a prolific and inspired technical author and magazine editor who founded a number of 'practical' magazines in the era that preceded today's 'do-it-yourself' movement. The key element of 'F J' was that nothing was beyond the ability of the dedicated practical man and he relished publishing material on how to build all manner of objects from cars to boat, dynamos, doorbells and radios. And, following the Flying Flea, he wanted to have another go at promoting the home-built aeroplane.

However, while this was an undoubted fillip for Latimer-Needham's design, it put enormous pressure on the little company to produce a set of working drawings for the aircraft. As revised for the magazine, the aircraft evolved into the Luton LA.4 Minor, having a taller undercarriage than the prototype and with parallel lift-struts in place of the V-struts of the original and a simpler tailplane and elevator.

Pre-War amateur construction

As the 1930s came to a conclusion, amateurs all over the country were reeling from the failure of the Flying Flea. Less than two years after it had published the Flea drawings, *Practical Mechanics* published the first of six monthly articles on how to build the Luton Minor. This appeared in October, 1937 with the last in March of 1938.

The recommended engine was the 32 hp Anzani, an Italian design which was produced in Britain by the British Anzani Engine Co of Scrubbs Lane, Willesden, London. The firm agreed to produce this for Latimer-Needham's use as the Luton Anzani, these two words incorporated into the crankcase casting.

Inspired by these articles in what was then a fairly prestigious magazine which told the enthusiast how to make almost everything and anything people up and down the country began making Luton Minors. Only one problem was to block them – the outbreak of war in September 1939 which put a stop to all private flying.

However, in the interim a number of aircraft had been started and several actually completed. The first to be finished and to fly was that constructed by James Stephen Squires. Started in 1937 and finished late in 1938, it was registered **G-AFIR** and fitted with a Luton-Anzani engine. It flew successfully at Rearsby in Leicestershire.

Also completed about this time was that of John Edmund Corine of Castle Drive, Douglas on the Isle of Man. Begun in 1938 and completed in just five months, it, too, was powered by a Luton-Anzani engine fitted with dual ignition and an impulse starter. Although registered **G-AFRC** it never carried these letters but flew unmarked being test-flown at the long-abandoned Hall Caine Airport in January, 1939 by an experienced pilot named Frederick Dodd, who did a lot of flying in the Minor.

Corine was an interesting man who effectively taught himself to fly on the Minor after only four

The prototype LA.3 Luton Minor G-AEPD with its Luton-Anzani engine being run-up with designer Cecil Hugh Latimer-Needham leaning into the cockpit to operate the throttle. Note that on this model the rudder bar protrudes from the lower nose of the fuselage and the cable-runs are all external. Also visible is the drag bracing wire running from the top longeron at the engine mount and forward pylon strut attachment back to the top of the forward lift-strut. The Anzani was a noisy engine devoid of any silencer as seen here.

Designer Latimer-Needham chats with the pilot as the first flight comes to an end. For the little cash-strapped company this was a major moment. The Anzani engine was small, compact, attractive (especially to owners of Morgan cars) but developed far more noise than justified its power output.

hours of dual instruction. His lack of experience did not diminish his enthusiasm for the machine and he wrote a glowing article on his Luton-Anzani-powered Minor which was published in *Practical Mechanics* that March – exactly one year since the final article on how to build the Minor was published. He described how he learned to fly the aircraft and how pleased he was with its performance. However, on March 12th, 1939, with Dodd at the controls, the engine lost power soon after take-off and the subsequent forced landing in a field a mile from the airport resulted in a broken fuselage and a damaged hedge-row. Before he could repair his slightly battered aircraft, war broke out and all civilian flying throughout the British Isles came to a halt.

Meanwhile Squires was having his own problems. The Luton-Anzani was not quite a fully reliable motor and he suffered several engine failures resulting in forced landings. As was found in the case of Corine's G-AFRC, it was prone to engine failure through blocked fuel jets. In the late spring of 1939 Squires had to cope with an engine failure above a very large and flat field of growing corn. His touch-down in the middle of the Leicestershire meadow at Hathern resulted in the aircraft turning upside down and causing a fair amount of damage.

Worse, however, was the reaction of the farmer who forbade any attempt at rescuing the aircraft until the crop was fully grown and harvested. Unfortunately it was a wet summer and the exposed fuselage sustained extensive water damage. By the time it was rescued in August 1939, repairs represented a major task.

On the outbreak of the 1939-45 war, Squires continued to restore his aeroplane in the hope shared by many people that the war would soon be over. By the time repairs were almost completed that winter Squires became resigned to the fact that it was going to be a while before civil aviation got going again. The Minor, now mostly finished, was stowed in the trusses of a corrugated-iron roofed garage in the middle of Barrow-on-Soar, Leicestershire. The troublesome engine was not re-fitted and, over the subsequent years, it was lost.

There was a third Minor which had been started by C F Parker of Pembroke in Wales. He made some unofficial modifications to the fuselage rear decking (he dispensed with the curved decking and substituted a flat-sided, angled deck rather like the later G-AGEP), called it the Parker CA-4 Parasol and registered it **G-AFIU**. There is no record of it being finished although there are some reports of unofficial flights after the war was over. It is believed, however, that this airframe was probably lost during the war.

Another machine was the work of William Sheppard Henry of Chronicle Buildings, Newtownards, County Down, Northern Ireland. Registered **G-AFUG** and designated the WSH.1, this was begun in 1939 and scheduled to be powered by a Luton-Anzani but, because of the declaration of war, it was never completed. The part-built airframe did not survive the war. However in the early 2000s a non-flying airframe was replicated and painted with this registration as a museum exhibit.

A further example was begun at St Margaret's Hope, Orkney. This was the work of W Petrie of South Ronaldsay and was registered **G-AMUW**. Begun in 1952, this was not completed but is allegedly in store on the island. These were all LA.4 pre-war-designed Minors.

A Change in Legislation

Since the emergence of private or civil flying as distinct from military aviation, the Government body charged with the responsibility of 'getting the paperwork right' was the Air Ministry.

The Air Ministry was created on January 3rd, 1918, to replace the organisation chaired by Lord Curzon known as the Air Board which in turn was formed on May 15th, 1916. This was responsible for the legislation associated with all devices that travelled in the air from balloons to the aeroplanes in the newly-formed Royal Air Force, itself created from the Royal Flying Corps (RFC) on April 1st, 1918.

Along with this, and by default, it had to look after the interests of civilian flying and privately-owned aeroplanes such as the De Havilland Moth or the Blackburn Bluebird. It was also responsible for the heaviest military aircraft, commercial public transport machines run by the many airlines and charter companies, and for anything else along the way such as those few small aircraft that didn't qualify for a full C of A and which flew on a restricted Permit to Fly.

It was an increasingly curious tie-up with fast and powerful combat biplane fighter aircraft on one hand and low-powered training machines on the other.

The 1939-45 war saw an immense increase in the development of aircraft while the first jet aircraft were tentatively touching our skies. Some four-engined heavy bombers gave birth to the first big long-distance airliners. It was a condition that demanded a wholly-different system to oversee operations. The Air Ministry had enough to cope with without the growth of civil aviation especially since its needs and administration were increasingly becoming slightly different from the operation of military flying.

Powered by a 40 hp ABC Scorpion flat twin, G-AFBP was the first 'proper' LA.4 Minor to be built by Luton Aircraft Ltd at Gerrards Cross. Pictured here on the grass patch behind the Phoenix Garage at Tatling End, this was the origination of all the first series of *Practical Mechanics* articles. It differed from the LA.3 insomuch as that it incorporated parallel lift struts and an extended undercarriage with side-mounted compression struts. It was largely through the enthusiastic persistence of the magazine editor, F J Camm, that the Luton company got its act together and produced a set of engineering drawings for the aeroplane that could be sold to other enthusiasts.

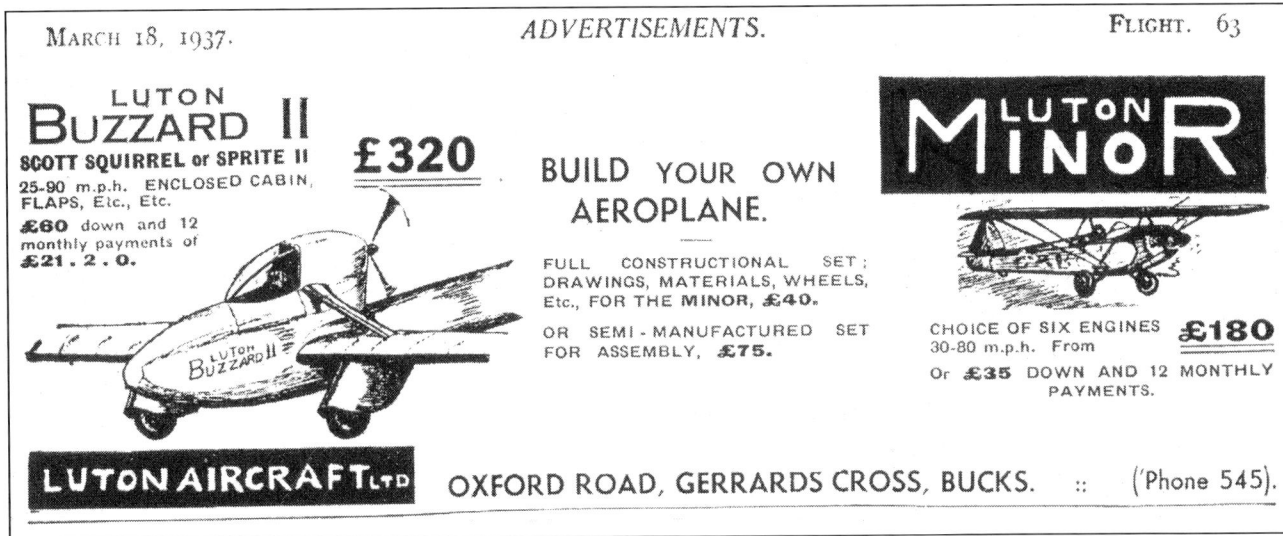

In those pre-war days, there was no 'Advertising Standards' organisation to control advertisers. It is a moot point whether Luton Aircraft Ltd's advert in *Flight* for March 18th, 1937 was really correct for despite the encouragement of Camm's magazine, it had little for sale. The advert gives the impression that Luton Aircraft must be a fairly large concern. Of course, it wasn't. The Buzzard powered sailplane had been broken and rebuilt to a shorter span, but was still very much in the experimental class. However, this advert put the company 'on the map'. Who knows what would have happened had war not intervened. To us today a flyable single-seater aircraft for £180 sounds a fair old bargain at a time when Tiger Moths and Bluebirds were between £300 and £500 depending on condition and engine hours as well as the length of the remaining C of A in months, normal validity being one year.

With the end of the war approaching, in August 1945 civil aviation was hived off with the formation of the Ministry of Civil Aviation. Eleven years later this would be revised as the Ministry of Aviation and later still it morphed into the Ministry of Transport. But it is the detail of the 1945 Act that was to seal the fate of the pre-war Permit system for home-made aeroplanes.

As it was created, there was no legislation to provide for the amateur aeroplane. Private and club aeroplanes with Certificates of Airworthiness Yes! Home-builts? No! The two bastions of flying didn't quite match up and the gap between them, small though it might have been, effectively marked finis to a part of aviation that involved the celebrated man in the street or, as he was oft referred to at the time 'the man on the Clapham omnibus'.

Home-made aircraft were frowned upon before the era of Henri Mignet, Now, however, they were positively discouraged. In fact, since there was now no legislation for them, they were simply illegal!

Days of the Doldrums

When the war ended in 1945, private and club flying resumed. It was stipulated that those pre-war aircraft that had operated on a Permit to Fly could apply for renewal. This was permitted so long as the aircraft conformed to some strict conditions. This was the poisoned chalice! The original airframe had to be used, any repairs or replacements limited to a maximum of 20 percent of the airframe. Crucially, the original engine had to be used. The aircraft had to have a maximum all-up weight not in excess of 1,000 lbs, a landing speed of no more than 40 mph, and a horsepower not above 40 hp.

Above all, the original documentation had to be available to corroborate its pre-war flight – certificate of registration, certificate of insurance, flying log-books and any maintenance records. On top of this there were some strict flight limitations including not flying over built-up areas, below certain heights and so on.

Most pre-war aircraft had been badly stored such that plywood had dried out or delaminated, spruce longerons had rotted and fabric had deteriorated. Some had contracted woodworm… That 20 percent new-build was invariably an unattainable goal since an airworthy aircraft usually meant a minimum of 80 percent new-build. And refitting unreliable engines, however original, would be suicidal. Better and possibly bigger engines made more sense but, while this sounded to be the responsible, safe way out of the problem, it was against the rules.

There was one exception to this ruling and it concerned an aircraft that was literally on its own in a unique situation. This was Luton Minor G-AMAW, a LA.4 model built to *Practical Mechanics* 1936 plans by Flt Lt J R 'Jimmy' Coates who lived at *The Spinney*, Heath Road, Breachwood Green, Hitchin. This was largely constructed during his RAF service which included time at RAF Stations Oakington and Waterbeach. He started it just after the war and registered it on October 3rd, 1950. Fitted with a 32 hp Bristol Cherub Mk.III, it flew extensively largely through a hole in the legislation and initially due to a highly-detailed Service inspection report by RAF engineers. Later named *Swalesong 1*, this aircraft is still flying.

Altering the Rulebook a bit

I had just come out of the Royal Air Force and completed my conversion-training for my Private Pilot's Licence. This in itself was all a bit of a big unknown. H\itherto flying licences for civilians were categorised as the 'A' Licence for private flying, and the 'C' licence for commercial flying. I was one of the first to receive the new Private Pilot's Licence.

Helping my friend Paul Simpson restore his first Aeronca got me interested in aircraft construction and restoration. Paul was a student at Loughborough College of Aeronautical Engineering, later to become Loughborough University.

Paul was in student digs at Barrow-on-Soar in Leicestershire and one day he happened across Squires Garage in the centre of town. Hanging from the rafters inside the corrugated-iron-roofed building was a rather battered Luton Minor. In hot summers it had baked under the tin roof, in the rainy season it got dripped on and in the Spring birds left their 'calling cards' on it. The airframe had no engine fitted, but there was a large cardboard box containing most of the parts of a French-made Moteur Mengin flat twin. The most valuable part, however, was the paperwork! Certificates of insurance and registration plus logbooks. Remember this was an age when paperwork could make or break an aircraft. If you had no paperwork for an aeroplane, then there was not a snowball's chance in Hell of getting it flying again.

To cut a long story short, James Squires, the builder and owner of the aircraft, wanted to dispose of it and had been asking £50. This was probably a fair price since he later revealed that the engine, dismantled though it was, had alone cost him £25.

Now, however, he wanted to get shot of it and halved his asking-price. In due course, £25 changed hands and I became the owner of a battered green and silver Luton Minor registered G-AFIR and a box full of bits of engine. Paul Simpson agreed to take the engine to his College and try to service the motor for me. In fact, Paul made many of the missing parts and spent many long hours working on the engine.

This motor had an interesting history. It came from the one and only Avion SCAL *Bassou*, G-AFCD which had crashed before the war.

The sad story of this twin-boomed pusher two-seat aircraft, originally registered F-APDT, plays a significant part in my tale. It was brought to England where it was impounded by Customs & Excise at Heston Airport. In August 1937 it was offered for sale by tender before being sold to 44-year-old Walter Louis Lewis of Richmond, Surrey. On June 12th, 1938, he took off on a local flight, stalled and dived into the ground, killing him outright. Being a pusher, the engine, a Moteur Mengin Model GMH two-cylinder horizontally-opposed affair, survived unscathed with its original highly-polished wooden propeller intact. Squires, looking for an Anzani replacement, bought it just as the war stopped all civil aviation.

Now it was at my home at Pinner, Middlesex. While the engine was now in fine working condition, it had lost its original magnetos, a pair of Sagas. Despite my best efforts of the time, suitable replacement mags were not available, nor were replacements to be found. I didn't have the skills or the workshop equipment to fit alternative mags which course of action one would take today.

On the matter of tools it is worth pointing out here that the average amateur constructor of this time (and this includes me) had only hand tools available to him. Even the now-common domestic electric drill was not available until the 1950s. Workshops and work were labour-intensive and tasks such as drilling split-pin holes through bolts had to be done by hand with a hand-drill – and an awful lot of spare drill-bits!

Although the Mengin fitted the Minor very well and I got as far as fitting it and making cowlings for it, I eventually had to admit that I would never get it to fly with that engine. Rated at 40 hp at 2,300 rpm and 54 hp at 2,550 rpm, it would have been a first-rate driver for the Minor.

One of my other interests was the Ultra Light Aircraft Association of which I had been a founder member. This organisation was created following a meeting of enthusiasts in London in October 1946. Six years later this would change its name to the Popular Flying Association, today's Light Aircraft Association.

But back in the 1940s my other associates in the ULAA were all mature ex-RAF and military types and I was by far the youngest member. This was to make for some occasionally bad chemistry because I tended to want to do things my way which was always at youthful variance with the way an ex-officer of the King's Air Force might approach things. I found the so-called proper channels slow and ponderous.

An enthusiastic reader of *Practical Mechanics* was James Stephen Squires in Leicestershire. He had already built a Flying Flea and now the magazine was promoting the Luton Minor. Squires was quick off the block and completed his example in record time. In fact, his was the first to be built. He registered it G-AFIR on August 14th, 1938 and started flying almost immediately. The earliest picture of this pioneering aircraft was this, taken at Rearsby in 1938 and showing it as a brand new aircraft with its large and rather ugly Luton-Anzani engine. The device at the top of the portside forward wing lift-strut is a Tiger Moth-type mechanical airspeed indicator consisting of a spring with a metal plate on it: the faster one flew the greater the pressure on the metal plate which carried a pointer on one end that showed your speed against a quadrant scale.

The ULAA had managed to secure a relatively large number of unused Aeronca J.99 JAP twin engines which had been built by J A Prestwich for the pre-war Aeronca. They had laid down a quantity for production only for Aeronca in Great Britain (they were at Peterborough) to go bust because the aircraft were proving more difficult to sell than expected.. The price of the engines was £80 apiece. I bought one, having first to form myself into a flying club to obtain a loan from the Kemsley Trust.

Seeking a British Aircraft for Homebuilders

It was France and French enthusiasts who really set the post-war amateur aviation scene. They had several fine designs that people all over France were not just constructing, but they were allowed to fly them! We had nothing – unless you count a robust anti-home-made aeroplane legislation.

France's Druine Turbulent, designed by the youthful Roger Druine, and the Jodel of designers Jody and Delmontez showed us the way to go – if we could. In the end both the Turbulent and, soon afterwards, the Jodel would be approved for construction in Britain but back in 1950 there was no British design approved for the likes of the frustrated home-builder. The ULAA looked for somebody to design a small aircraft that could be built by ordinary people from a set of plans.

There were two men who seemed to fill the bill – John Britten and Desmond Norman on the Isle of Wight. Both were graduates of the de Havilland Technical College at Hatfield where they had met and established a close friendship.

Forester Richard John Britten (1928-1977) was the quiet, reticent type, possessed of a nervous twitch of the eyebrows but a good aircraft designer. Nigel Desmond Norman (1929-2002) was ex-RAF Reserve by this time. They had formed the unofficial firm Britten-Norman, later incorporated as a limited liability company in 1954. Their interests were in crop-spraying in foreign parts where there was money to be made in the burgeoning area of agricultural aviation.

Through Grp Capt Edward Mole of the ULAA, the two men were approached to see if they could come up with a lightplane design. This was in 1950.

With the aid of a close friend who had worked on John Britten's family estate at Bembridge – a talented woodworker named Peter Gatrell – work started on the B-N1F, a single-seater powered by one of the ULAA's JAP engines. The aircraft incorporated a number of unusual features, among which was a central wing flap that extended between port and starboard ailerons, a short fuselage – and a box-section welded cantilever undercarriage secured on each side of the fuselage by fourteen quarter-inch bolts. The wing had no internal drag bracing. Instead alternate pairs of ribs were boxed over with 1mm plywood to create torsion boxes.

Everybody looked at the B-N1F with enthusiasm for it was so different from anything else we in Britain had ever flown. Upon its completion, Desmond Norman took the controls of G-ALZE for the first flight at Bembridge Airport on May 16th, 1951. It did not fly quite as expected tending to wallow. In other words, directional control was poor and the margin between take-off and cruising speed was much smaller than hoped for.

Desmond never quite got as far as attempting to verify the undoubtedly high stalling speed because, on the third flight, a blocked fuel jet caused engine failure soon after take-off. In the ensuing landing on rough ground outside the aerodrome perimeter, the smart undercarriage was torn off, its robust 14 quarter-inch bolt attachments each side not proving adequate to the plywood and spruce fuselage which snapped clean in half at the cockpit.

Gatrell built a whole new fuselage, this time fitted with a conventional V-strut-braced landing gear and powered by a 55 hp Lycoming engine. The wings were extended in span and the fin and rudder increased in size. The problem, though, was that once you try to improve something which is not perfect the result is really no more than a patch – a makeshift solution. As it was, the revised B-N1F was not a good flyer and all the improvements actually contributed to a worsening of the handling.

The ULAA was now concerned that its quest for a British lightplane design was no nearer. I decided that this was a situation that required some sort of quick solution so I sat down at my drawing board in Pinner and designed a very simple light aircraft that was capable of using the stock of engines held by makers J A Prestwich. The result was a simple and compact design which I named the Wee Mite. It was designed to be built in a garage or large shed – or a sitting-room if needs be.

A scale model was built and successfully flown at Pinner and Grp Capt Mole thought it was worth proceeding with.

However, reality soon began to kick in. A wholly-new design would cost money to get through Air Registration Board design approval and we just didn't have either the cash or the time. It was then that I realised that we already had a thoroughly tested design – the Luton Minor. Here was an aeroplane that flew well, that we had all the paperwork for and one which could be updated to provide a low-cost answer to our quest.

In the late 1940s, the Ultra Light Aircraft Association, forerunner of today's Light Aircraft Association, desparately sought a British design for the new generation of home-builders. We had two French designers but we needed an all-British one – one of our own! John Britten and Desmond Norman dreamed up the B-N1F which looked fine on paper. It crashed in early tests and a new version was built, seen here. This second-stage Britten-Norman B-N1F with its robust strutted undercarriage, extended wing span, larger rudder, added fin area and 55 hp Lycoming engine was still not a good flying machine. After a few trial flights which confirmed a lack of directional stability – and the subsequent addition of tailplane 'zulu-shields' like the DH.86B Express, the Britten-Norman design was dropped and the ULAA's encouragement – such as it was – transferred to the Luton Minor.

The ULAA was placing much store on the success of the Britten-Norman B-N1F built at Bembridge Airport in 1949-50. After the third-flight crash of March 1950 which broke the fuselage in two, a second fuselage with more robust landing gear was made. But there were still fundamental problems with the design and directional stability was only one of them. Grp Capt Mole, who had put up with many comments and observations from me, invited me to produce a design. Pictured at my drawing board in Evelyn Drive, Pinner, I got down to work designing the O-H7 Wee Mite to fill the ULAA need for a British

design for home-building, Quite a way down the design process, I came to my senses and realised that this was not the best path to our goal and that it would be a far better proposition to take an existing pre-war design and modernise it. Such a re-design was more like to be approved than a whole new enterprise. In terms of expenditure, it would be cheaper to get past the Ministry of Aviation and the Air Registration Board. This was the real moment that the Luton LA.4a Minor was born.

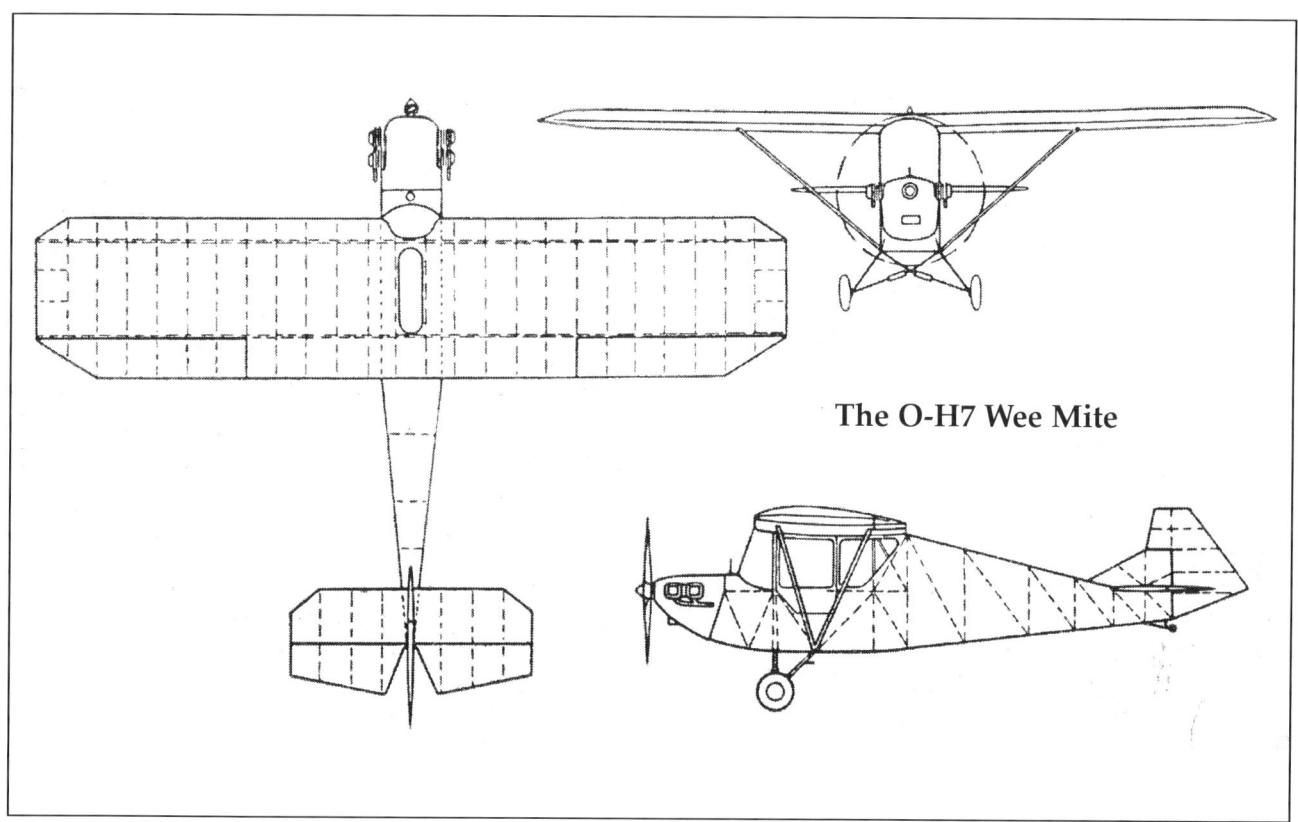

The O-H7 Wee Mite

At the end of the 1939-45 war, the urge to build your own aeroplane soon re-emerged. All that was available were two French designs – the Jodel D.12 and the Druine Turbulent. When the executive committee of the Ultra Light Aircraft Association, soon to be renamed the Popular Flying Association, decided it ought to have an all-British design to help kick-start the home-building movement in Britain, John Britten and Desmond Norman had been invited to come up with a solution. Their answer, the Britten-Norman B-N1F, was an over-engineered aircraft that was a bit short on good flying qualities. The Association's youngest member, one Arthur Ord-Hume, came up with this, the O-H7 Wee Mite – very basic, very simple and easy to build. But there was a better design staring everybody in the face. Flown pre-war, approved by the old Air Ministry and with plans already circulated to the masses via a popular magazine. It was called the Luton Minor… The basic airframe of the O-H7 was built as a training exercise by the Harrow Air Training Corps but never completed.

The outcome of the struggle to produce a British design was the restitution of the pre-war Luton LA.4 Minor and the first off the blocks were Ron Miller with G-AGEP, Ted Felce with G-ALUZ, Flt Lt Jimmy Coates with G-AMAW – and a real old-timer – the very first example, G-AFIR rebuilt by me. Here is the restored 1938 aircraft now fitted with a British-built Aeronca JAP engine and a tailwheel.

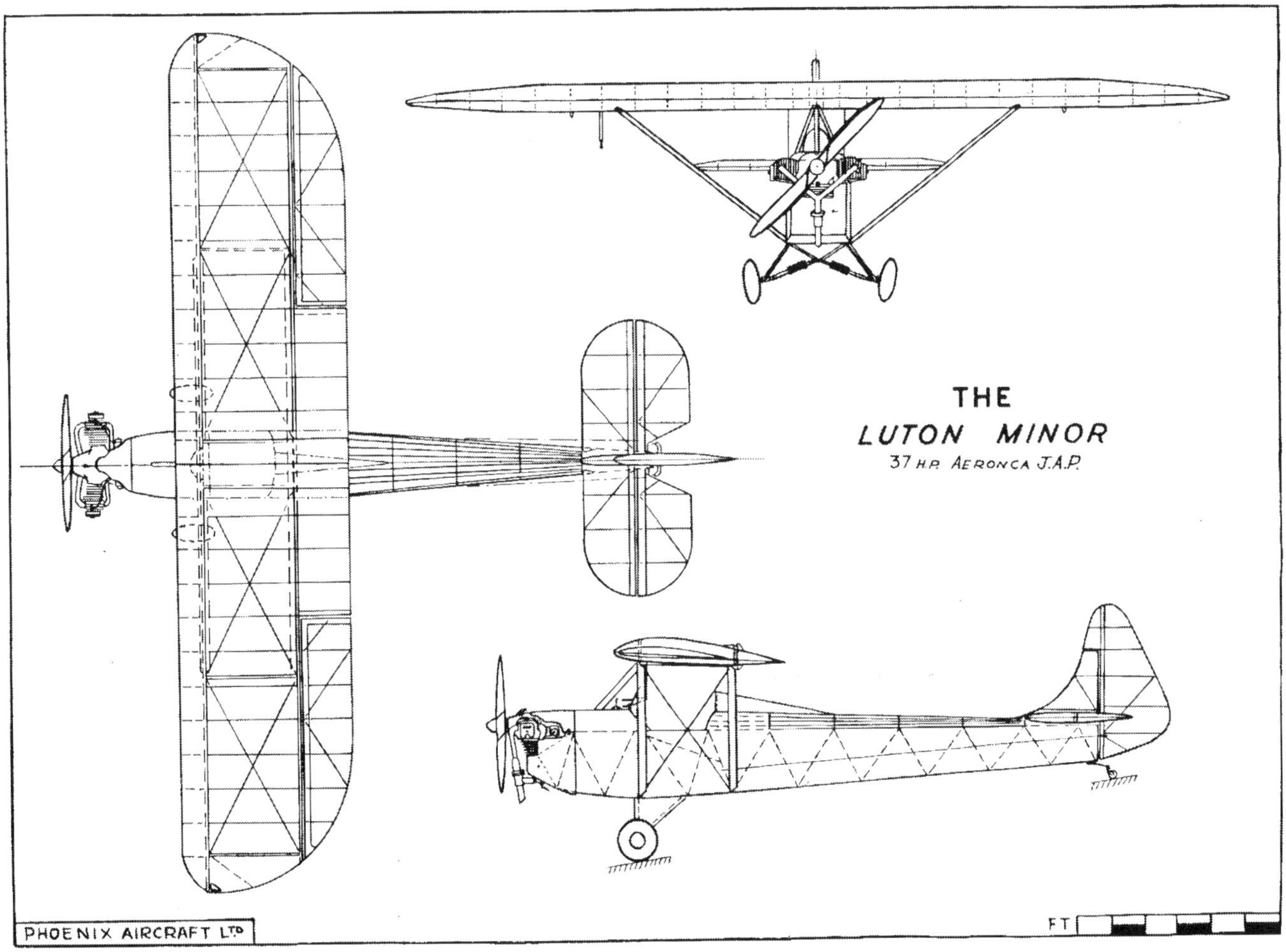

THE LUTON MINOR 37 H.P. AERONCA J.A.P.

While flying LA.4 Minor G-AFIR extensively, I embarked on the re-design of the airframe to create the LA.4a seen here in this three-view. The notable changes are the shape of the fin and rudder allowing internal cable runs for the elevators, the revised extended undercarriage and two-piece wings with box spars in place of the slender plank spars of the pre-war version. There were many other detail changes to improve construction and performance.

A far cry from the LA.2 and LA.3, the LA.4a looked like an aeroplane – and flew like one. All who tackled it commented that it was a little on the slow side but flew like a dream. G-ASEB was built by J A Anning in Leeds and first flew at Yeadon on May 4th, 1963 powered by a Lycoming 55 hp flat four engine.

The Luton Minor gets a re-vamp

The original designer, C H Latimer-Needham, was at that time living just outside Bognor Regis at a place called North Berstead. I telephoned him and introduced myself as a Luton Minor owner and explained what the ULAA, shortly to become the PFA, was all about and what we wanted to do with the aeroplane – modernise it and sell it as sets of plans to enthusiasts to build their own examples. Latimer-Needham's words were not encouraging. He was rather off-hand and said he saw no value in 'throwing good money after bad' and that the aircraft design had been overtaken by the war and that he was not interested.

The upshot was that I considered this rebuff as an assertion that he just was not likely to cooperate. I set to on my own and began updating the 1936 design. I had heard that Latimer-Needham's philosophy was to restrict welding to an absolute minimum as he could not afford the necessary gas. Which is why the old Minor has a few metal fabrication quirks.

The cumbersome undercarriage of G-AFBC gave way to a properly-braced landing gear fitted with wheel brakes. Gone were the slender plank wing spars in favour of I-beams and box-spars, and there were many other details that updated the old design.

During this time Latimer-Needham moved to Wonersh in Surrey and, in order to keep things running smoothly, I reckoned it was important to form a company to handle the project and there was some value in having the original designer on board,. Once again I approached him and this time he invited me to his new house. Eagerly I rolled up all my drawings for the 'new' Minor and headed for the Deer Park private estate at Wonersh where, in a house named *High Oaks*, Latimer-Needham had moved with his wife.

Phoenix Aircraft is Founded

Presented with what I had devised as a sound business plan, Latimer-Needham's attitude changed completely. I think he saw that I was not just some kind of threadbare nut, but that I meant business. Now he was positively enthusiastic. The upshot was that in 1958 together we formed Phoenix Aircraft Ltd with him listed as chief designer and myself as managing director. These were positions I had carefully worked out as likely to speed the process of design approval. The name came from the Gerrards Cross factory at Tatling End. This had been called Phoenix Works and, in 1943, it had burned down while machining magnesium in the presence of water. Rebuilt as the Phoenix Garage and no longer anything to do with aircraft, we took the name as 'rising from the flames'. Incidentally, his brother, Eric Needham, ran the garage right up to his retirement at at the age of 89. Only closing because Shell would no longer supply fuel, claiming that it sold less than than the required contract quantity.

Classified as the Luton LA.4a Minor, the updated Minor had good looks and was simple to build and fly. Sets of plans were sold all over Britain, many to the United States and a surprising number to Australia and New Zealand. The post-war *Practical Mechanics* articles on construction are referred to as the 1960 set.

Throughout this time I was also working on crop-spraying aircraft, and as well on hovercraft. We launched the Minor and began selling sets of plans. All was going well and while Latimer-Needham

---

ULTRA-LIGHT AIRCRAFT
Obstacles Deliberately Put in the Way

THE letter from Mr. E. J. Pope (*Flight*, November 7th) is typical of the troubles experienced by many other enthusiasts who are building their own low-powered aircraft and those who wish to fly them. It would seem that obstacles are deliberately put in the way of those who should receive encouragement and help.

I am afraid that the A.T.C. and the R.A.F. won't receive many volunteers when it is realized that they won't be able to make and fly their own little aircraft later on.

The "Magna Charta" of low-powered aircraft building and flying is the Gorell Report, and any attempts by Ministries to infringe the rights then granted should be fought tooth and nail in Parliament.

The whole matter was most thoroughly investigated at the time and a safe arrangement made.
ERIK T. W. ADDYMAN
(Hon. Sec., The Aircraft Club).

Luton-Minor and "Permit to Fly"

WITH reference to the letter of E. J. Pope in *Flight*, November 7th, it may interest him to know that I, also, built a Luton-Minor, just before the war, finishing it, in fact, too late to receive permission to fly.

Since my return to "Civvy Street" from the R.A.F. I have been in communication with the Air Ministry regarding a "permit to fly," but have been given to understand that ". . . it is by no means certain that it will be possible to reintroduce this pre-war practice."

I take it that this must apply to all ultra-light types, and wondered just how many enthusiasts have been similarly grounded by this edict.

I have flown the machine twice—permit or no—and found it very sweet to handle, though a bit underpowered with the Carden engine.

A "permit to fly," even with all the pre-war restrictions, is all that I want—C. of A. is too expensive—but I want it now, not at some vague, very future date, and I can see no sound reason for its refusal.
T. N. WALKER.

At the end of the 1939-45 war, there remained a small but vociferous number of pre-war aircraft owners and builders who had operated on the special Permit to Fly system. This also allowed home-made aircraft to be flown. However, changes in legistlation now excluded home-made aircraft from this system. Correspondence in the magazine *Flight* revealed that there were many aircraft owners who had slipped through the net and had aeroplanes that they were prohibited from flying. These two letters, above, appeared in the issue for December 5th, 1946. Erik Addyman was a noted prime mover in northern aviation circles at that time.

largely lived in retirement, I ran Phoenix Aircraft from my home at Lake on the Isle of Wight and a shared drawing office with my other business, Agricultural Aviation Co Ltd at Panshanger evolving crop-spraying and crop-dusting equipment.

The newly-formed Popular Flying Association now had three designs, two French and one British, to promote to hopeful home-builders. Soon we would be joined by a fourth – the Currie Wot biplane, another British pre-war design updated for the post-war market.

Phoenix Aircraft goes sour

All good things eventually come to an end and the collapse of thriving Phoenix Aircraft came about in an unrelated way. I had taken an interest in hovercraft and, in particular, was contributing articles to a newly-formed technical magazine called *Hovering Craft and Hydrofoil*. Among other things, such as working with the original hovercraft designer, Christopher Cockerell (1910-1999), I was at pains to try to increase the altitude which the average hovercraft could attain. I referred to this height as 'measureable with a dip-stick' and bemoaned the fact that hovercraft operated in a sort of play-pen environment easily restricted by small objects. In truth the maximum height above the ground was usually no more than about six inches.

It was at this point that I invented the flexible skirt for hovercraft. As my business partner, I thought nothing of explaining my design to Latimer-Needham and demonstrating this, showing him my model flying in the confines of the blister hangar which formed my Panshanger base. I discussed with him how the flexible skirt could be made in inflatable segments enabling obstacles to be crossed with ease. He was very interested in this.

It later transpired that virtually the next day Latimer-Needham had taken out a patent on my invention. Now that would have been fine if it had been in the name of Phoenix Aircraft or even Agricultural Aviation. Unfortunately, it was not. It was in the sole name of Cecil Hugh Latimer-Needham of *High Oaks*, Deer Park, Wonersh, Surrey.

I was naturally rather disturbed by this, especially when I found that he had immediately sold the rights to the patent to Saunders-Roe which paid him £1,000 for each of the hovercraft subsequently built and fitted with 'his' skirts.

It was as a direct result of this breach of trust that I dissolved our partnership on the terms that I retained the rights to the Luton Minor and the two-seat variant, the Luton Major. It was an unfortunate day when this happened because the fellow was an important character in his own right and his actions did not seem to fit his reputation. Shortly afterwards he retired properly, going to live with his daughter in Canada where he later died. Phoenix Aircraft Ltd experienced a flurry of hopeful directors but none contributed anything and the business was wound up soon afterwards.

Prologue

Everybody who flew the Luton Minor spoke highly of it. Yes, there was a lot of aileron drag but the stall was docile and the controls light. It's an old design now. Even the post-war redesign is now seventy years into the past. However, if somebody wants a simple aeroplane to build and fly, then the little Minor is still a candidate. Today the choice of engine is larger than in the days of the 1950s and '60s with the converted VW being one of the most popular of the 'oldies'.

The larger two-seat LA.6 Major had a less fortunate time. Because so many of the original drawings were destroyed in the wartime fire at Phoenix Garage, Gerrards Cross, I had to re-stress the entire aircraft. In so doing, I increased the all-up weight to 1,150 lbs. Later, and without reference to me, the then engineering officer of the PFA allowed a Major to fly with an all-up weight in excess of 2,000 lbs.

The owner of the aircraft contravened the primary condition of the Permit to Fly which states that aerobatics are prohibited – this fact is placarded on the instrument panel – and proceeded to fly a series of loops with a result that was as predictable as it was terminal. A fine aeroplane thus assumed a bad reputation. Interestingly, several other Luton Majors built to my updated plans are flying on the Continent and in Australia where they are behaving very well at the specified all-up weights to which I designed the airframe.

This book, then, is the story of the Luton Minor told in pictures with detailed captions. It is also the tale of Luton Aircraft Ltd and its successor, Phoenix Aircraft Ltd. It also relates how the aeroplane became the first British design to get approval for home-construction.

A question may be asked as to what happened to G-AFIR? As a historic aircraft, it ought to be preserved. It had its last rebuild at the hands of Arthur Mason of the Vintage Aircraft Club. Completed and almost ready to fly, he passed it on to another who did little other than lose bits. More recently it seems to have gone into limbo but no doubt it will be found by another generation of more appreciative enthusiasts whereupon it will probably end up in a museum or even Shuttleworth!

To end with, one other aircraft carries the names 'Phoenix' and 'Luton'. This is the so-called Phoenix Duet. Originally known as the Minor III, the Duet is a side-by-side two-seat version of the Luton LA.4a Minor, designed and built by Grp Capt Alfred Stanley Knowles 'in association' with the former Phoenix Aircraft Ltd. Design began in 1968 and it was registered G-AYTT on March 4th, 1971. It really isn't anything to do with Phoenix Aircraft or even the old Luton company. We thought of a two-seater Minor quite early on and this was called the LA.8 Minor Two. It was never proceeded with.

Knowles' aircraft was a private venture that sat two side by side. The Duet flew for the first time two years later, on June 22nd, 1973, and qualified for a special category CofA on June 24th, 1974. During 1976 square-shaped wing-tips were developed for the Duet, and flight testing with these began in early 1977. The new tips increased the wing area, and resulted in reduced stalling speed, increased rate of climb and improved gliding angle.

Finally a quick word about another aircraft prefaced with the name 'Luton'. When in 1964 Rollason sponsored their *Miniature Racer Competition*, one if the contenders was a small group who designed a nifty little speedbug called the Beta, They called themselves the Luton Group and their sole purpose was to compete in the contest. All credit to them – but they were nothing to do with Luton Aircraft Ltd or Phoenix Aircraft Ltd.

Some of the pictures in this book are of very poor quality but they are included for their importance or rarity. It is fair to state that the Luton Minor was largely responsible for kick-starting post-war home-building in Britain and the variety of aircraft turned out in amateur workshops up and down the country was quite impressive.

Bibliography

The reader will gain wider knowledge of the type of work involved in building a light aircraft by reading the book *The First Home-Built Aeroplanes* (Ord-Hume, published in 2009 by Stenlake), This book reproduces in facsimile the three series of *Practical Mechanics* articles devoted, first, the Henri Mignet's Flying Flea, then to Luton Aircraft Ltd's Luton LA.4 Minor, and finally to Phoenix Aircraft Ltd's LA.4a Minor.

Flt Lt Jimmy Coates' Cherub-powered LA.4 Minor was built to the pre-war *Practical Mechanics* instructions and was completed by him in the RAF which made it much easier for him to fly it since it was considered to be between civil and military jurisdiction! I went up to RAF Waterbeach in Cambridgeshire to see his progress on one occasion and we posed his aeroplane with a much larger Dakota with vaguely amusing results that raised thoughts of feeding time... His Minor, named *Swalesong*, would inspire him to design and build other aircraft. Meanwhile his LA.4, registered G-AMAW, became a regular attendee at PFA Fly-Ins and is now to be found in the Light Aircraft Association's own Museum collection.

Tales of interrupted construction due to the outbreak of war are legion at this time. Many a half-built aircraft went into store never to appear again. One candidate for this scenario was the Luton Minor which a Seaton, Devon, man, L R Miller, built from a Luton Aircraft Company kit of parts. His construction actually started in 1942 and by mid-1944 his handiwork looked like this. However in 1952 it was sold to the air-race handicapper and former RAE aerodynamicist John Arthur Bagley (1929-2003) who later became senior curator of the aeronautical collections at the Science Museum. He stored the Minor at Farnborough until C M Roberts took over the project in 1959. But G-AGEP was destined for a short life and its wings were donated to the Gowland Jenny Wren, G-ASRF.

Unlike other Luton Minors of the mid-period, Flt Lt Jimmy Coates' G-AMAW was a success, largely possible by the fact that his little run-about was allowed to fly under the unofficial auspices of the Royal Air Force. Adopted by the Popular Flying Association (now the Light Aircraft Association) it is a frequent static display machine at the annual gatherings. Although it has not flown for a while, it is a reminder that our beginnings were in simpler times.

Pictured by Allan Wooller at a rural setting in Hastings, New Zealand, this was one of the first NZ Minors to be built to Phoenix Aircraft plans by Kip Netherclift. In the early post-war days of civil flying, all New Zealand aircraft had registrations preceded by the national letters 'ZK' until somebody with a saving in paint in mind, realised that virtually all small aircraft in New Zealand were quite incapable of 'international flight' – in other words leaving New Zealand's luscious hills and flying to, say, nearby Australia (4,155 km). From then on it became legal only to display your 'last three' – in this case, 'CLL'.

A very early British Luton LA.4a Minor built to Phoenix plans was G-ATFW built by schoolmaster George W Shields of Mexborough Grammar School. First flown at Hemswell in Lincolnshire and fitted with a four-cylinder Lycoming A-145-A2 and subsequently based at Doncaster.

The other aircraft associated with Luton Aircraft Ltd.

The Luton Buzzard was the first of Cecil High Latimer-Needham's designs to be built by the Luton Aircraft Company Ltd at Barton-on the-Clay airfield, Bedfordshire. It was more of a powered sailplane than a light aircraft. Originally conceived as a product of Latimer-Needham's sailplane business Dunstable Sailplanes Ltd, the Buzzard was Luton Aircraft's first product to be prefixed 'Luton'. With a wingspan of 40 feet and an all-up weight of 800 lbs, this open-cockpit single-seater first took to the skies at Barton-in-the Clay, Bedfordshire, in 1936. Registered G-ADYX it was powered by a 35 hp Anzani inverted V twin. Unusual feature was the one-piece all-flying tailplane. From the US magazine *Popular Aviation* for December 1936 comes this view of the sole example. Designer Cecil Hugh Latimer-Needham stands on the left. It was promoted as the £325 aeroplane but did not sell.

The Buzzard was quite an attractive aeroplane. The long, slender tail-boom was constructed as a plywood monocoque. This was a bit of a weak link as the shock of a tail-down landing could easily snap off the tail. On the approach, the all-flying tailplane/elevator tended to over-correct movements of the control stick. This problem was reported by almost all the pilots who flew the aircraft – and that was about four!

The other aircraft associated with Luton Aircraft Ltd.

Although it was designed to be powered by the 32 hp Scott Flying Squirrel, the Luton Buzzard only flew with the Anzani engine. This followed a chance meeting with the manager of the British Anzani company who saw an opportunity to market a large number of motors through Luton's designs. Neither knew that the country would soon be at war and civil aviation would cease for five long years. And neither quite appreciated that the Anzani was not the most reliable of motors available. To help clinch the deal, Anzani undertook to make special front-face engine castings replacing the sole word 'ANZANI' with the couplet 'LUTON-ANZANI'. Not that this improved either sales or performance. Using sailplane-inspired high aspect-ratio wings, G-ADYX was a good flyer although the engine noise from the unsilenced twin-banger was too loud for comfort. Here the Buzzard takes to the air for the first time. Note the open cockpit and semi-cowled engine. Photograph by *Flight*.

The Buzzard was provided with split flaps and an all-flying tailplane. This latter device was something of a 'nine-day wonder' at the time. Tried out on other, conventional sailplanes, it had the advantage of being lighter and cheaper to manufacture but the downside was the extreme variations in stick forces needed to alter the tailplane angle in flight depending on speed and attitude. While ideal for some sailplanes (and later jet fighters) it was a dubious feature of the LA.1.

The other aircraft associated with Luton Aircraft Ltd.

The Luton-Anzani engine installation in the original first version of the Buzzard G-ADYX. The wide pulley that substitutes for a propeller spinner on the rear of the propeller is for a starting rope as inspired by the Belgian-designed single-seat Tipsy monoplane. Starting the engine by hand-swinging the propeller while leaning over the fuselage tail boom would have been a bit hairy. Wrapping a rope round this pulley allowed one to turn over the engine without being anywhere near the propeller.

On November 16th, 1936, the Buzzard was severely damaged when it hit trees following engine failure on take-off. The mishap took place at Christchurch Aerodrome after which the remains were dismantled and taken back to Barton by road. It was rebuilt with extensive modifications as the Mk.II Buzzard with shorter-span wings, enclosed cockpit and a conventional fixed tailplane and separate hinged elevator. Now with a wingspan of 35 ft 6 ins and an all-up weight of 600 lbs, the Mk.II had a closed cockpit, better-cowled engine and a revised undercarriage. It carried the same registration and first flew in 1937 but, on May 8th, 1938, while being demonstrated at the Royal Aeronautical Society Garden Party staged at Sir Richard Fairey's Great West Aerodrome (later to be London Heathrow), it was damaged beyond repair. The remains of the aircraft were taken back to Luton Aircraft's factory at Gerrards Cross where, while machining magnesium castings during the war in 1943, fire destroyed the premises and all the stored aircraft said to comprise the prototype Luton Major plus six incomplete Major fuselages, the prototype Minor and the remains of the Buzzard. This picture of the Mk.II Buzzard was taken by E J Riding at the Garden Party an hour before its terminal crash.

The other aircraft associated with Luton Aircraft Ltd.

During 1938, the threat of war with Germany seemed inevitable and as a result of this on July 23rd, the Secretary of State for Air Sir Kingsley Wood announced the formation of the Civil Air Guard. Its purpose was to provide pilots who could assist the Royal Air Force in a time of emergency. A suitable training aircraft had to be selected. Latimer-Needham saw his chance and came up with a tandem two-seater design, the LA.5 Luton Major. The prototype G-AFMU, was built at Gerrards Cross and powered by a 62 hp Walter Mikron Mk.I inverted four-cylinder inline engine.

A very youthful Harold Best-Devereaux (1919-1985) decked out in 'plus-fours' prepares to work the switches while a colleague gets ready to swing the propeller in this picture taken by *Flight*. The Luton Major was an attractive-looking aircraft and the sole prototype first flew in March 1939. Test pilot was Group Capt Edward L Mole. This picture was taken by Edwin Riding in the summer of 1939. Luton Aircraft's hopes for 'a massive order' as a Civil Air Guard trainer were, of course, out of the question. Already maintenance demands for hard-working trainers were stipulating a far more robust structure than Latimer-Needham dreamed up for the Major. Furthermore, it was stipulated that the entire aircraft had to be of British origin: the engine for the prototype was made in Czechoslovakia.

The other aircraft associated with Luton Aircraft Ltd.

The prototype LA.5 Luton Major, G-AFMU, takes to the air in March 1939. In spite of grand hopes for a major production order (which Luton Aircraft Ltd would not be able to meet) this would be the only one built pre-war. Latimer-Needham's dream of its selection as the official training aircraft for the Civil Air Guard was a challenge too great even for his wildest hopes. For a start, it did not have that vital commodity for a CAG trainer – a British-made engine. The motor as fitted to the sole Luton factory Major was the four cylinder in-line Walter Mikron I made in Central Europe – already hotbed of uncertainty as the 1939-45 war drew ever closer.

After the war and after the restoration of the Luton Minor by the newly-formed Phoenix Aircraft Ltd, thoughts turned to the LA.5 Major. So little remained of the original aircraft drawings that the machine was designed using photographs as the only source of material on the original aircraft. It proved to be a long and arduous task involving a complete new stress analysis but finally all was completed and the company began selling sets of plans. One of the first to be completed was this one, G-BCKP. Styled the LA.5a. this one was fitted with the 65 hp Continental engine. Built by J Callow at Barnwell, it was completed in June 1977 and is pictured here at Popham on September 13th, 1992.

The other aircraft associated with Luton Aircraft Ltd.

Because almost all the original drawings were lost in the Gerrards Cross fire, design of the post-war Luton Major was largely a new project. The few surviving pre-war plans had an interesting journey to my drawing office in Shanklin on the Isle of Wight. Latimer-Needham was a sailing enthusiast and had a small boat which he kept in the Lymington area. He said he would come and see me on a certain date and deliver the surviving charred paper remains by sea. It was a rough evening and he was unable to risk attempting to make landfall in his boat. He turned up the next day a bit dishevelled, having spent the night at anchor in Sandown Bay with the portfolio of precious papers. In the end, much of the original design detail was illegible and useless. The new Major became the LA.5a and here is an early example, G-ASWH, built by S G and T G Stott of Wincanton. Powered by a Walter Mikron II, it first flew in February 1965 at Compton Abbas and gave good service until a handling mishap on July 3rd, 1977, after which it was withdrawn from use.

A nice picture of the two-seat Luton LA.5a Major climbing out of Compton Abbas in 1968. The Major was surprisingly quiet in the air, almost regardless of the engine.

The other aircraft associated with Luton Aircraft Ltd.

Constructional drawings for the post-war Luton designs were marketed around the world by Phoenix Aircraft. Numbers of sets of drawings went to Australia where the first to be completed and to fly there was this one, VH-EVI, in 1973. Fitted with a Continental 65 hp and painted white and red with black letters, it undertook extensive flying until the owner retired it and donated it to the Australian Aviation Museum at Bankstown. Like so many of these important museums, this one has been closed recently and the whereabouts of its exhibits is unknown.

Built in Switzerland and resident there, HB-YAH is a much-travelled Major and has visited the Popular Flying Association rallies on a number of occasions, notably Cranfield in 1994 and Sywell in 2007.

First off the mark in those distant pre-war days was James Stephen Squires of Leicestershire who was the first to complete his Luton LA.4 Minor to the instructions in *Practical Mechanics*. One of the earliest pictures of James Stephen Squires' G-AFIR was this one taken in 1938. The aircraft is fitted with the 40 hp Luton-Anzani inverted V twin-cylinder engine. This picture was published in the magazine 'English Electric and its People' for April, 1952. Squires, born about 1909 and died 1980, worked for English Electric back in the 1930s. This historic example became mine when £25 changed hands in March 1949. During the 1939-45 war, Squires was a Home Guard pilot and a gliding instructor.

Loaded up from Squires Garage in Barrow-on-Soar, Leicestershire, the fuselage sat on a four-wheeled trolley. This proved very difficult to drive with as the wheels were not castoring. A short distance into the homeward journey we ditched the trailer, turned the fuselage round and towed it on its own wheels. The wheel bearings, not intended for running miles on pre-motorway roads, kept overheating, necessitating repeated stops on the way home to be reoiled. The tyres also took a pounding and we got through four layers of canvas by the time we were home. It was well past midnight when we reached Pinner. Paul Simpson drove his mother's car while I sat on the open sun-roof giving hand-signals and shouting instructions to Paul. It was a very cold journey!

First rig at Evelyn Drive as G-AFIR sits on the back lawn. In its pre-war colour scheme as repaired for resumed flight which never came, the fuselage was green and white, the wings silver and red. On the rudder was the diamond-shaped trademark of Vigzol, an oil refining company founded in Ormskirk, Lancashire, in 1919 as a manufacturer and distributer of motor oils to local farms and garages. In 1924 it opened offices in London's Manhattan Wharf and a second production facility in Dublin. Vigzol was founded on hard work and enterprise with a desire to provide better and better lubricants. No foreign capital or interests have ever been associated with Vigzol. The company developed its sales in one field – agriculture – to an extent where it claimed to lubricate the majority of farm machinery, before selling itself to Amoco International in 1962.

My good friend Paul Simpson worked hard on the Moteur Mengin and I spent many hours installing it. A nice engine, it cowled very well and suited the Minor perfectly. The only problem was that sometime during the war years it had lost its twin Saga magnetos. It was impossible to obtain replacements, on top of which the Ministry and the Air Registration Board were not keen on approving the engine. I was told that I must refit the recalcitrant Luton-Anzani. With the airframe rebuilt and, as seen here in the front garden of my parents' house, flight not being too far away, I was informed that there was no way the Mengin would be accepted. I was forced to scrap all our engine work and buy and fit one of the ULAA's new Aeronca-JAP engines.

Just about every photographer over a radius of tinkety-plonk miles about wanted to visit and get his own pictures of this home-made plane in a front garden at Pinner. Most of them were just trying to earn an honest living and I went along with it. Only one reporter sent me reeling towards my typewriter to demand from his editor an apology in print and this was a fellow who, having interviewed me alone one afternoon, published a story with added dialogue from an imaginary wife who wasn't present. He was a disgrace to an otherwise decent bunch of chaps upon whom I was to lean heavily at a later date.

One of the problems of building an aeroplane in domestic surroundings back in the 1950s was that it was considered very novel and extremely newsworthy which meant that every newspaper in the land wanted its own individual pictures of the activity. For me it was a waste of time. If it took a photographer half a day to take his pictures, that was half of my day wasted. But there was another agenda and that was that I knew the publicity was going to do the amateur aircraft movement a lot of good. And the more the Ministry of Aviation was prodded with this sort of publicity the sooner (one hoped) they would realise that home-built aeroplanes were here to stay and they would have to do something about it. I just had to put up with it. Without delays because of filming and photography, getting the aircraft airworthy would have been far quicker but without the publicity it would have been a far steeper climb through officialdom. Many of the Committee of the ULAA and later PFA disagreed with me, but in the end I was proved right. Here I am posed trying to poke a screwdriver through an engine crankcase – it made the front page of some contemporary newspaper.

Our family home at Hatch End, Pinner, back in those post-war years was a rented property on what was at that time a private estate. Few people owned their own houses in those days. Our estate agents were a bit snobbish about what you could get up to on their exclusive bit of rural Middlesex and fairly high up on the list was building aeroplanes. Since it was not unusual to have cameras and cameramen taking pictures of all that I did and since these photographs and stories were published fairly world wide, keeping quiet about what I was doing in my front garden was not easy. While back gardens were one thing, activities in your driveway were not easy to hide. It turned out that building an aeroplane was not the sort of activity to be encouraged. Here is a copy of a letter my father received during the work on G-AFIR.

In the garden at Evelyn Drive, my friend Dick Potter of Bourne End, Buckinghamshire, poses in G-AFIR with his wife, always known as Bubbles. Dick started to build a Minor with a Carden-Ford engine at his home but, following a horrendous motorcycle accident, he was forced to dispose of it unfinished to Howard Shore of Ryde who used the engine and propeller in a surface skim boat he built.

With the new and untried JAP engine in place, it became necessary to see if it ran OK. We rushed the fuselage to the unfinished spur of road a few doors down. Here the engine had its first run. Kevin J Crooks is in the cockpit working the throttle. Douglas Marr stands starboard side watching while I click the shutter. It is early 1950 and in time to come the field in the background would be my occasional airstrip. It's all built up now.

The rebuild of the pre-war Minor G-AFIR was completed by the beginning of April, 1951. We towed it to Elstree Aerodrome behind Paul Simpson's old car, ASR269. Here it is loaded up outside our house in Evelyn Drive. The beam across the rear bumper made a fine and secure position to attach the fuselage. Wings could be carried this way as well. One problem with modern cars is that they are almost impossible to use for towing aircraft. You cannot even attach a decent roof rack!

Ron Cole captured for the magazine *Aeronautics* one of the big moments at Elstree as, with my team of helpers, I attempt to first engine-start after rigging the machine at the airfield. At the wing-tip is Douglas Marr, later to become a Red Arrows' pilot in the RAF. Almost out of sight at the other side of the cockpit is Angie Chiesa and the chap looking technical and charged with working the throttle is Robin Vincent. Both the last-named were apprentices at Handley-Page and Angie was, some years later, destined to own the aircraft after I had sold it.

G-AFIR sits thoughtfully on Elstree's grass. The spinner, said to have been a source of inspiration for a latter-day pop-singer's foundation garments, added a touch of zest and zip to the top speed which was off the scale. Initially the Airspeed Indicator (ASI) didn't read low enough. Top speed was in the order of 80 mph and the stall was at about 30 mph.

On the day of the first flight, I invited all the photographers and reporters whom I had met over the years to come out to Elstree – and watch me break the Law because my aeroplane had no Permit to Fly. I sent a copy of my 'press release' invitation to the Ministry of Civil Aviation. There was a good turn-out that particular morning, including a rather nervous copper from the local constabulary who was told he was to arrest me when I landed. Just before my 'first flight' took place, a messenger arrived by motorcycle with my Permit to Fly. The first flight? Oh! That was the previous evening and consisted of half an hour of sheer joy! Gentlemen of the Press! I salute you, the chaps who helped shame a Government Ministry!

My reconstruction of the very first LA.4 Minor flew well and I had several good hours of flying in the red and silver machine. There were very few adjustments needed. I was then due to return to my RAF station so I filled up with fuel and put the aircraft back into one of Elstree's hangars. Six weeks later I returned for some more flying, normal pre-flight checks and then I was away. Nobody had alerted me to the 'dirty fuel' scare at Elstree while I was back at my RAF station. Apparently, there had been several instances of aircraft suffering engine failure the previous month. Elstree's petrol tanks were examined and found to be contaminated. Now they had been drained, cleaned and refilled. I had a tank full of the old stuff and it caught up with me on May 1st, 1951. My forced landing at Carpenders Park was influenced by the proximity of the railway line and a forest of telephone wires on the embankment with the result that I had to make the best of a rough field full of large ant-hill tummocks. I had managed to break poor old 'gaffa' pretty thoroughly. Farmer Hedges kindly loaned me his tractor and a flat-bed waggon to get the bits back to Evelyn Drive. The *Watford Observer* took this picture. It was May 1st, 1951.

Some wit suggested that brass handles and silk sheets would round off my own special box. The new fuselage sitting on the grass outside my Panshanger workshop was surprisingly light and one could demonstrate a strong-man act by picking it up at the middle and carrying it around. I chose to rebuild the aircraft as original – an LA.4 – but with those modifications and improvements that I had incorporated in the *Practical Mechanics* articles.

My efforts to rebuild my broken G-AFIR were largely charted by news reporters who regularly came out to Hatch End for the day and spent their time (and mine) moving things around for their cameras while I was prevented from working. This picture, a United Press photograph, was taken on January 24th, 1953. It was syndicated around the world and was noticed in America, Australia and South Africa. And, as I was about to find out, by our worthy estate agents again. The warning, printed on page 34, was now a bit more sharpened… People on private estates simply did not build aeroplanes. So there!

After rebuild number two, Paul Simpson's car was no longer available but a friend of mine at Handley Page stepped into the breech. Here in May of 1956 – cherry-blossom time – we tied the new G-AFIR on to Johnny Tank's car, AVX 157, for the slow tow to Elstree's aerodrome.

Starting the JAP engine was, usually, very easy. Only once in a while did it prove difficult. So when Charles E Brown, the ace air-to-air photographer, turned up at Elstree to get some pictures of me dancing with the clouds, we had an unfortunate bit of dancing in the grass to sort out first.

The renowned aerial photographer Charles E Brown was a friend of mine. On several occasions I had flown one of Elstree's Austers for him to use as a camera plane, the last one being a year or two earlier when the first Druine Turbulent came over here, so when G-AFIR was flying again after my second rebuild, he said he would like to do some air-to-air photography for Oliver Stewart's magazine *Aeronautics*. This is one of the pictures he took from Auster G-AGXT at Elstree on September 22nd, 1956. Elstree Flying Club's chief instructor, Bill Bailey, piloted the Autocrat.

Having concluded a good aerial shoot, photographer Charles E Brown took a final picture at Elstree after we had landed. While the other pictures did credit to the little aeroplane, publication of this one in Oliver Stewart's magazine *Aeronautics* this one was a bit unflattering. It showed the result of having a lot of hair and flying without a helmet and goggles.

Flying from Panshanger to Sandown on one memorable day, a heavier-than-predicted thunderstorm came in from the west and gave me a turbulent headwind all the way with the result that I found myself between Petworth and Midhurst and low on fuel. I estimated that at my present rate of knots I would run out of petrol somewhere over the middle of the Solent. Beneath me lay the inviting meadows of South Mead Farm, Tillington. I landed and was met by the farmer's children. The farmer gallantly drove into Petworth to get me a jerry-can of fuel. The downside was that I had no cash on me and in those pre-credit card days, he had to trust me to refund him by post. Which I did the instant I got home. Date of event? August 5th, 1956. Those children will be in their seventies now.

My first wife was June Brenda Windust, younger daughter of Spitfire-designer R J Mitchell's nurse at the end of his life. Here she sits on the grass at Sandown Airport with our son, James Edward, and G-AFIR. In the background, top right, are the original airport terminal buildings and clubhouse. Jim later went on to rebuild Spitfires and Me109s before working on hovercraft.

After this the second rebuild (or was it three?) it was almost four years since the LA.4 had been broken at Carpenders Park. Now it was flying again with almost an entirely new airframe. This embodied a number of modifications that had suggested themselves during the previous use and construction. I did a fairly extensive amount of flying in her and everywhere we went those camera shutters clicked.

Luton Minor G-AFIR visited many places in the 1950s and 1960s. Here it pairs up with Jack Cosmelli's unique Hirtenberg HS.1A, G-AGAK, at a now-forgotten destination.

Not satisfied with the small-fry (Ansons and so on), the Luton Minor gives scale to G-AHFB, an Avro York at Luton Airport.

Richard Webber with his LA.4a Minor, G-BRWU, when he flew into Sywell to meet the author in 2017. Richard, who owns Eggesford Airfield in Devon, is also a well-known Auster aficionado.

A line-up of LA.4a Minors at the Popular Flying Association's Sywell fly-in. From right to left, G-AXKH, G-AVDY and G-AZPV.

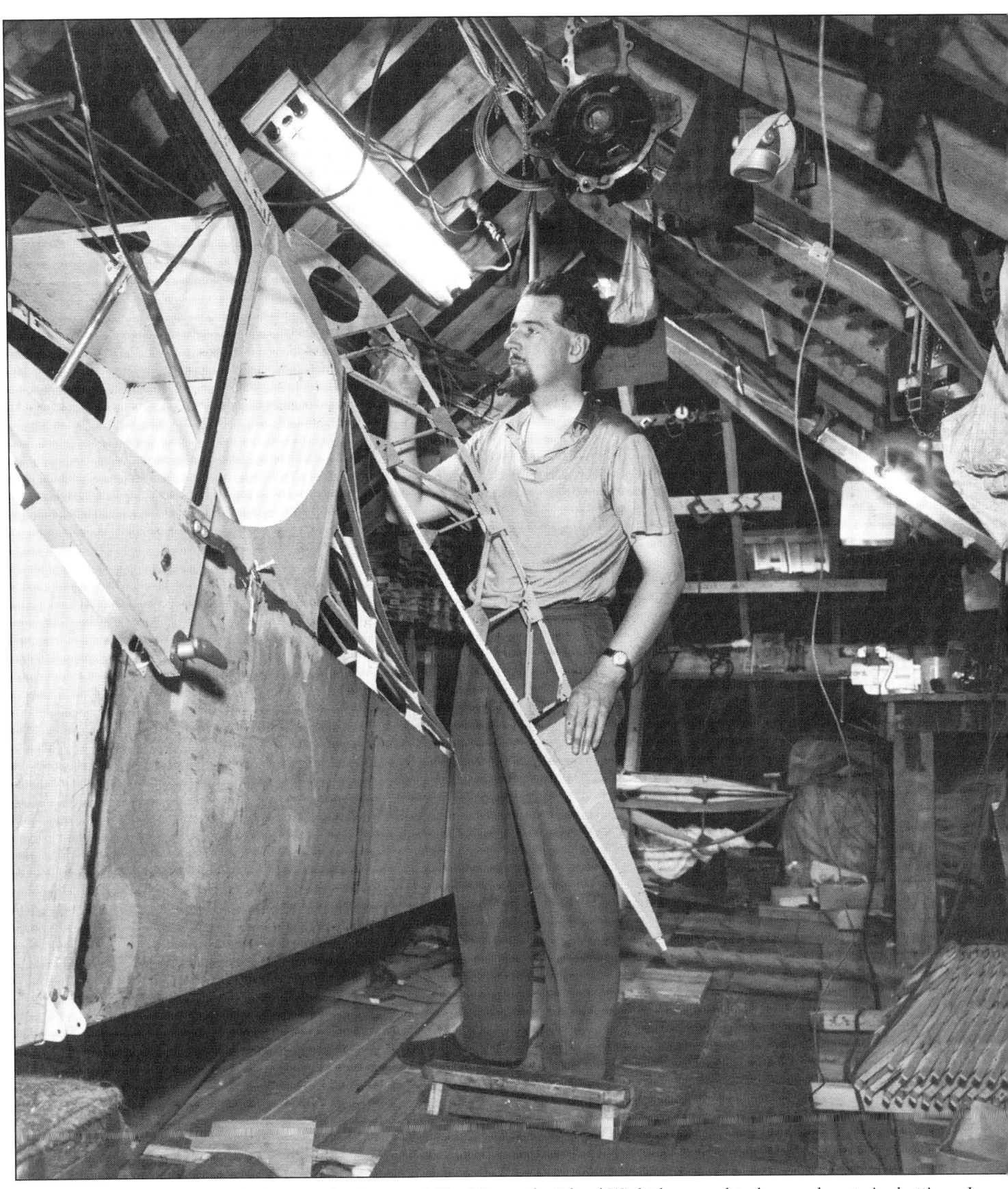

My bungalow at Lake between Sandown and Shanklin on the Isle of Wight happened to have a decent sized attic so I converted it into a workshop. Floored with driftwood, the conversion was cheap and here I built several aircraft, among the a 1938 LA.4 replica, G-ASAA, and the prototype of the Cabin Luton Minor, the O-H6.

I spent many long hours in my attic at Lake but it was convenient and made an excellent workshop that was not dependent on weather or transport. These pictures were taken by Charles Everest with whom I would work quite closely in years to come. Anything that required photographing from the air – ships, places, Ryde's Theatre Royal when it went up in flames, the roll-out of the first Saunders-Roe Hovercraft – we would be there with a carefully positioned Auster and then we would fly the film to Southampton/Eastleigh for that night's TV news.

Removal of a bundle of roof slates and two half rafters provided a fine opening through which one's handiwork could be removed. Fuselages were lowered gently onto the lawn where they could easily be transported into my specially-built twenty-foot long garden shed.

One of my creations in the attic was this LA.4 registered G-ASAA. Mostly completed at Lake, with the aid of a couple of friends we pushed it on its own wheels to the hangar at Sandown Airport where it was completed, the finish being white and light blue with yellow cheat lines. The considerable time spent on the finish proved worth it when I attended the July 29th 1963 PFA Rally at Rochester and won an award for the best-finished aircraft on the field!

When it was decided to build another Luton Minor at Sandown, the result was a hybrid making use of a fuselage that I had built some years earlier at Panshanger. G-ASAA was theoretically an LA.4 but fitted with two-piece wings built around the box spars of the LA.4a, an improved LA.4 undercarriage and a special 1927 Stag Lane colour scheme. The overall colour scheme was light blue, white and a dark blue cheat line. It is pictured here at its roll-out at Sandown Airport prior to its first test-flight on July 29th, 1963. The engine is the 37 hp Aeronca J.99 JAP.

The author poses with G-ASAA at Sandown Airport. The manual choke control for engine-starting is just visible in the lower main engine-cowling as a small round grommet in line with the cowl vertical edge. Pulled out before starting, this little lever could be pushed back in again once the engine was running; alternatively it was closed automatically when the throttle was opened fully.

Test-flown by me on August 28th, 1966, G-ASEA was constructed at Wellesbourne near Stratford on Avon by constructors Grahame P Smith and M Fawkes. First flown on September 27th, 1967, this Aeronca J.99 JAP-powered Minor was built in a former chicken-run at Lapworth. The lady fondling the fuel filler cap is Penelope Torrance, one of my test-flight helpers.

Tom Reagan built G-AWIP at Crawley in Surrey. It made its maiden flight at Redhill Aerodrome in 1970. It is powered by a Continental C65-8F and carries the name 'Sarah'. The picture is posed for a local news photographer but, having been at the receiving end of this sort of thing for many years, I can forgive him!

Reagan's Rolls-Royce Continental-powered LA.4a Minor was finished in a very smart paint job. In 1988 the aircraft sustained damage in a forced landing due to engine failure caused by a blocked fuel filter.

One of the earliest home-builders to the revised drawings for the LA.4a was William Charles Hymas in Kent. His G-ARXP was first flown in 1966 powered with a 37 hp Aeronca J.99 JAP engine but later he re-engined it with a four-cylinder in-line Walter Mikron III as pictured here.

Mike Vaisey was a leading light in the Luton Minor revival and gathered together a 'squadron' of similar aircraft that used to fly the rounds of air shows. His machine, G-AXKH, was built at Hemel Hempstead and was first flown at Panshanger Aerodrome on June 22nd, 1974. The engine was the ubiquitous Volkswagen VW.1,600 cc flat four.

Quite a few Luton Minors were built in Australia where Walter J Watkins had founded the Ultra Light Aircraft Association of Australia back in 1956. This association altered its name in the mid-1970s to the Sport Aircraft Association of Australia. JAP-engined VH-RPH was built in 1962 and since 1993 has belonged to Cary William Button. It is seen here being prepared for its first flight.

When Richard M Sharphouse of Thirsk, Yorkshire, built G-ATCJ he decided to go the whole-hog and alongside the aeroplane he built this handsome trailer in which the complete aircraft could be stowed and transported. One wing can be seen leaning against the left side of the trailer. The aircraft first flew at Dishforth on September 1st, 1972. It spent its initial years at Bagby and later moved north into Scotland.

Originally constructed at Dunstable by S A Knight, he was forced to pass G-BBEA on to G J Hewitt and J B Stocks at Peterborough for completion. Powered by a VW1500 Peacock conversion, it first flew at Connington in 1975.

An unusual Minor was G-AVLX built by Noel Frederic O'Neil and Robert Stephenson Parker of Belfast. This was fitted with a neat enclosed cabin top and first flown at Newtownards in June 1968 powered by an Ardem 4002-1. Sadly it didn't last too long being allowed to overturn in a gale.

Built in Sheffield by John Tallent and Ian McNeill, G-AVDY was fitted with a Lycoming O-145-A2. It first flew at Tollerton on April 22nd, 1967. Colour scheme was red and white. This was one of the founding members of what came to be known as 'The Luton Minor Group' which won a prize at the Sherwood Flying Club at Tollerton in 1967.

Engined with a Volkswagen VW 1834 and built by R J Parkhouse, this LA.4a Luton Minor G-BKHR was first registered in August 1982.

A popular sight around air shows is G-ASML which is powered by an Ardem 4002-1. Begun in 1963 it first flew in 1966. Flown by Barbara Schlusser, the registration has generated the aircraft's nickname – Gasmantle! Not too many people around today will know what one of those is…

Many aircraft have nick-names. My old Luton Minor was Gaffer – the slang term for 'boss' or chief. The Luton LA.4a Minor's registration G-ASML generated the nom-de-plume Gasmantle after its letters. Here Gasmantle demonstrates its steep climb-out with 55 hp from its Lycoming engine as pilot and owner Barbara Schlusser takes off.

The 1939-45 War interfered with many homebuilt projects. R S Finch of Darwen started his Luton Minor from *Practical Mechanics* articles in 1937 but had to store the incomplete airframe through the war years. Construction and registration (as G-AHMO) was briefly resumed in 1946-49 but it went back into store. Finally, with an Aeronca JAP engine, it was sold to T G Thompson of Cottesmore and started flying from Rearsby. On October 22nd, 1966, an attempted short take off out of wind at Sandown Airport proved too much for the venerable one-seater and she crashed in a close-by field. The remains were incorporated into G-ATWS.

Unauthorised alterations to an approved aircraft designs are not encouraged! In fact, all builders are instructed to stick to the drawings implicitly. Any changes have to be thoroughly vetted by the Light Aircraft Association or the original designer otherwise it will result in an expensive and painful slapped wrist. But once in a while something comes along that's different and interesting. This was the work of one William Mason of Kent who modified his aircraft so that it could be towed on its own wheels behind his family car. Having examined his idea very carefully, his system, which involved major changes in the wing attachment geometry, appeared eminently practical and, subject to a proper and thorough stress analysis, probably perfectly adequate. He constructed his aircraft and it was reputed to be complete and ready to fly when the 1939-45 war broke out. What happened to Mason after the war is not certain, but his aircraft re-appeared in the early 1980s in a warehouse somewhere in South London where these photographs were taken. In this view is the added drag wire which extends each side of the nose from the top longeron at the engine mounting bracket and runs to the top of the front lift strut. A rectangular door each side of the cockpit is provided to accommodate the centre-section when it is rotated 90 degrees for wing-folding. The engine is the J.99 Aeronca JAP meaning that this was the very first instance of a JAP engine installed in a Luton Minor. At that time it would have represented a novel and modern powerplant. No registration markings were ever allocated or applied to the airframe.

This picture was taken in 1939 by a local newspaper and shows William Mason in his living room working on his special Luton Minor with his son Jack while his wife, Doris, appears to be applying fabric to a wing in the background. Mason was employed in the panel-beating shop at Short Brothers in Rochester before and during the Second World War. His son Jack also worked there at the same trade. William Mason developed a method of beating out the leading edge of a Sunderland flying boat wing in just four hours – a task that hitherto had taken a fortnight. Consequently, because he was paid on a piece-work basis, his earnings were relatively high. At home, he chose to construct a Luton Minor in his spare time. However, he appears to have spent some considerable effort revising the structure prior to starting. His idea of a 'swivelling wing' required basic alterations to the fuselage structure in the cockpit region and in this picture son Jack is seen working on the square cockpit door into which recess the rotated centre-section could fit. In the fullness of time his wife Doris undertook all the fabric covering. Son Jack would later become a bomber pilot during the war.

The construction team pose with their special folding-wing'd Luton Minor with Short Brothers' William Mason, left, and sons Don and, right in RAF uniform, Jack. Note the V-shaped lift-struts folded flat under the starboard wing and secured with a catch. The 1939-45 war broke out on September 3rd – the very day that William Mason completed his Minor and this picture was taken. Having learned to fly on Moths at West Malling, Mason planned the Minor's progress thoroughly. However, despite being armed with his Pilot's 'A' Licence, all civil flying was prohibited so his plans to tow the aircraft to Rochester Airport for its test-flight had to be scuppered. William decided to hang on to his aircraft until after the war when he planned to take to the air in his unique Luton Minor. However, the return of peace in 1945 brought in new restrictions on private aircraft and he found that he was prohibited from flying his own aeroplane. This was not an uncommon outcome and Mason was one of the many who found that having a home-built aeroplane was anything but a 'licence to fly'.

The Mason Minor's wing-folding is a unique and clever system built around square centre-section front pylons replacing the original triangular one. To this is attached a rectangular fuselage centre-section. The aft part of this centre section is hinged so as to lift up and fold forward. In this view, the wings and the centre-section are in the 'flying' position. Each wing panel was hinged at the top at both main and rear spars so that when the entire wing and centre-section was rotated the leading edge pointed upwards and the wing panels could fold backwards. In this picture, the folding trailing-edge flap of the centre section is in the flying position.

To fold the wings, the forward drag wires, explained in the first picture caption, are disconnected as are the V-shaped lift-struts at their lower ends. The centre-section trailing-edge flap is folded upwards and over and locked to the front portion. The attachment of the centre-section to the rear centre-section pylon is also disconnected, and the whole wing rotated through 90 degrees so that the centre-section folds down into the cockpit: this explains the presence of the two cockpit doors, one each side to allow clearance for the wing.

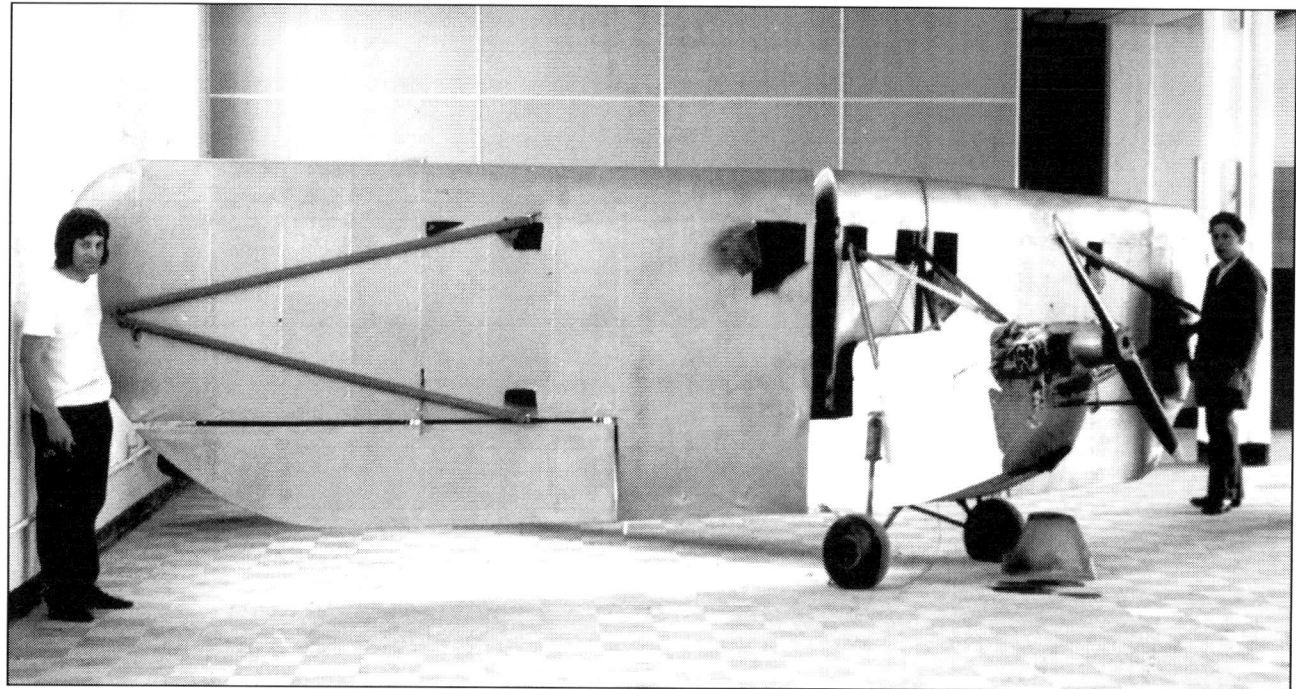

Here we see the curious geometry of the wing-folding with the wings folded down chordwise. Hinges on the top surface of the centre-section now allow the wings to be folded backwards. The lift-struts are also folded backwards to be locked in place at the underside of the wing-tips. It is mentioned in a pre-war write-up that Mason made his rudder with a trailing edge formed neatly from a continuous length of duralumin. This highlights the skill of the builder, the facilities open to him and adds credence to the probability that his employers took an interest in his spare-time work.

The completion of the folding process results in a very handsome appearance. It is believed that Mr Mason must have engineered this very closely for it is altogether a clever modification. The circumstances of the photo session seen here are strange. I received a call to my London office on a date in around 1970 as a result of which I was picked up from my premises by a taxi and taken 'somewhere' that was in the Catford area. After spending about half an hour with the aircraft and two men on the second floor of an otherwise empty warehouse, I was driven back to my office with the promise of further contact. Crucially I did not establish the address to which I had been taken – and I never heard again from either of the two chaps! This aeroplane is probably still out there somewhere.

CF-OVZ is one of the Canadian-built LA.4a Minors. Strikingly coloured dark blue and light blue, this is powered by one of the London-made Aeronca J.99 JAP engines and is based in British Columbia.

G-ASEA was one of the earliest LA.4a Minors to be constructed. It was the work of G Smith and M Fawkes who built it in a converted chicken run near Wellsbourne in the Stratford-upon-Avon area in Warwickshire. Here the fuselage is complete in red primer and the Aeronca JAP engine is installed. Subsequently I carried out some of the test-flights on this in September 1967 at Wellsbourne, a former RAF airfield six miles east of Stratford.

Don G Peacock of Colchester built his Luton Minor single-handed and was one of the first to reach post-war completion, making his first flight on August 15th, 1965. Power was provided by a Lycoming O-145-A8.

Don Peacock's aircraft was beautifully finished in white with registration letters in red.

Berwick is a close-by south-eastern suburb of Melbourne and here we find one of the more colourful of the Australian-built Luton Minors. Powered by a British built Aeronca JAP engine, VH-RFT first took to the skies in 1974. Describing the design in a 2015 review, local writers Roy Beiswenger and Marnio Boric said of the Minor 'it has a great deal of period charm and gives a back-to-basics fee, although performance doesn't match [that of] more modern designs. Predictable handling and sturdy construction make it a joy to own. A white scarf is a compulsory accessory'.

An interesting Luton LA.5a Major is this one, EI-CGF, registered in Ireland. First registered as G-ARWX, construction was begun in 1962 at Forres, Scotland, by A G Cameron. After two years of work he was forced to abandon the project so it was It is now registered EI-CGF and painted all white with red cheat lines and bold black registration letters. The engine is a Lycoming O-325. An unusual feature is the addition of a long-range fuel tank between the undercarriage legs. An idea borrowed, perhaps, from Rearsby?

Built by P Lea and E Lindgard of Sudbrooke, Lincolnshire, G-ASXJ was fitted with an Ardem 4002-1, one of the early conversions of the VW car engine. Later it was refitted with a Lycoming O-145-A2 flat four engine.

Somebody's small miscalculation? A Luton Minor being built in a suburban garage suggests a few future problems for the constructor, perhaps?

A number of LA.4a Minors were built abroad. Among the far-flung corners of the Earth that became home territory to my little 'two-banger' was America where a dozen or so were under construction at one time. This one, N4762T, is the handiwork of Robert Ryburn of Atwood, Illinois. Powered by an American-made Aeronca E-113C – the original motor that was licence-built in Britain as the Aeronca J.99 JAP – this first flew in 1967. Another US-built Minor was made by Dick Sheren of Grand Ledge, Michigan. He fitted his with a 55 hp Lycoming flat four.

In August 1965, Robert Ryburn's LA.4a Minor flew for the first time. That November he wrote me a glowing letter. 'As of now [the aircraft] has been flown by eight pilots. All of them are amazed by the wonderful handling characteristics, short turning circle, good climb-out and short landing run. Some of this flying has been done in 18-20 mph winds. I flew N4762T for the first time last Sunday and enjoyed myself thoroughly. The little ship is everything that I expected and is the easiest airplane to fly that I have ever flown.' Praise indeed!

Although Luton LA.4 Minor G-AGEP was registered just at the end of the war, its construction had begun in 1939. It was built by L R Miller of Seaton, Devon, and fitted with an Aeronca JAP J.99 flat twin. It differed from the usual models built from *Practical Mechanics* in that the rear decking of the fuselage was angled instead of being rounded. In 1952 it passed to John A Bagley at Farnborough and seven years later to C M Roberts. It then passed to Jack Gowland who rebuilt it as a one-and-and-half seater so he could take his small son flying with him. Re-registered G-ASRF and renamed the Gowland Jenny Wren, this Lycoming-powered tricycle-undercarriaged derivative was a regular visitor to many air events of the sixties and seventies.

Hard to believe but this aeroplane started out as a Luton Minor, Ron Miller's pre-war LA.4 G-AGEP was registered in September 1942. G W 'Jack' Gowland had an air-minded small son and decided that the Minor was a good starting point for a special one-and-a-half seater. Built at his home in Brookmans Park, Hertfordshire, Gowland used the modified wings off the Minor mated with a new fuselage. This had a jump-seat behind the pilot for his little boy. He called this tricycle-undercarriaged 55 hp Lycoming-powered hybrid the GW2 Jenny Wren. The closely-cowled engine was provided with exhaust augmenter tubes. Span was 27 ft 4 ins and length 21 ft 6 ins and the all-up weight was 900 lbs. First flown at Panshanger in September 1966, it cruised at 70 mph.

Once a regular flier around the light aircraft shows, Jenny Wren G-ASRF is now said to be in store awaiting another lease of life.

In Australia, the Luton Minor enjoyed a marked success with builders and at least a dozen were built and flown while one reliable source advises that at least three others were built and flown successfully without having gone through the paperwork process… VH-AYP is one that did. Built in 1963 at Sydney's Bankstown Aerodrome, it is seen here awaiting a propeller. Like most of the Australian-built Luton Minors, this one was powered by an Aeronca engine. Unlike most, however, this was powered by an American-made E.113-C with single ignition. Interestingly, to cope with local airfield management requirements, this example has a steerable tailwheel fitted.

Staying 'down-under', this fine example of an LA.4a Minor was built by Kip Netherclift at Napier in New Zealand and first registered on September 18th, 1974. ZK-CLL was powered by a 37 hp two-cylinder Aeronca-JAP engine and is pictured at Porangahau in 1978. In June of 2003, builder Kip sold ZK-CLL to K Garrett and R Naylor of Havelock North. It was then sold on to M H Kindon of Rangiora during May of 2005 and he then passed it on to Mike Fleming, also of Rangiora in November 2007. Later that month it was redesignated as a Class 1 microlight. One other LA.4a in New Zealand is worthy of attention and that is ZK-FSU. It was originally G-APVI and was imported into New Zealand by J T Hayes of Boston, Lincolnshire. Mr Hymas had been one of the original Luton LA.4a Minor customers for a set of plans. It was first registered in New Zealand on February 5th, 1989, and was based at Rotorua in 1989. Hayes sold ZK-FSU to Tony Rawlinson of Inglewood on November 6th, 1995, who still owns it.